Simply Put:
A Study in Economics
Student Book

Catherine McGrew Jaime

Catherine Jaime did her undergraduate work at the Sloan School of Management at the Massachusetts Institute of Technology. She has additional economics training through the Foundation for Teaching Economics and the Foundation for Economic Education. Catherine has taught grades K-12 with a concentration in high school economics and government. She has authored a number of history books and several booklets dealing with government and/or economics. She firmly believes in the importance of the U.S. Constitution and the free market, and it shows in her writings.

Copyright 2013, 2015 by Catherine McGrew Jaime
www.CatherineJaime.com

Creative Learning Connection
8006 Old Madison Pike, Ste 11-A
Madison, AL 35758
www.CreativeLearningConnection.com

Preface 5
How to Use This Book 6
Introduction to Economics 7

Lesson One - The Law of Unintended Consequences 9
Lesson Two – The Role of Prices 11
Lesson Three – Understanding Needs, Wants, and Incentives 14
Lesson Four - Elasticity of Demand 15
Lesson Five – Entrepreneurs and Opportunity Cost 18
Lesson Six - The Constitution and Economics 19
Lesson Seven – Important Economic Philosophies 24
Lesson Eight – Money, Money, Money 27
Lesson Nine – Standard of Living 29
Lesson Ten – Greed, Self-Interest, and Profit 31
Lesson Eleven – Division of Labor 32
Lesson Twelve – The Evils of Machinery? 34
Lesson Thirteen - Markets 36
Lesson Fourteen - Capital and Capital Goods 37
Lesson Fifteen – Voluntary Exchanges and Free Trade 39
Lesson Sixteen – Capitalism vs. Socialism/Communism 40
Lesson Seventeen – Central Planning:
   Individual Knowledge vs. Collective Knowledge 42
Lesson Eighteen - "Middlemen" – Meddlesome or Useful? 44
Lesson Nineteen – Speculators and Farmers – Friend or Foe? 46
Lesson Twenty – The High Price of Interest Rates 47
Lesson Twenty-One – Property Rights 49
Lesson Twenty-Two – Rule of Law 51
Lesson Twenty-Three – What's Fair? 53
Lesson Twenty-Four – Public vs. Private Services 57

Lesson Twenty-Five – Cost, Size and Role of Government 59

Lesson Twenty-Six – Disastrous Debt and Deficits 61

Lesson Twenty-Seven – Risks and Uncertainties 63

Lesson Twenty-Eight – Competition vs. Monopolies 65

Lesson Twenty-Nine – Government Intervention through Price-Fixing 67

Lesson Thirty – Minimum Wages 69

Lesson Thirty-One – Price Gouging 70

Lesson Thirty-Two – Rationing & Black Markets 73

Lesson Thirty-Three – Unemployment and Unions 74

Lesson Thirty-Four – International Trade and Outsourcing 76

Lesson Thirt-Five: = Recessions, Depressions, Inflation, and Staglation 77

Lesson Thirty-Six – Too Big To Fail? 80

Conclusion 82

Review Questions 83

Economics Mid-Term 97

Economics Final Exam 99

Appendix #1 Wealth of Nations: Division of Labor 101

Appendix #2 The Pilgrims Try Communism 104

Appendix #3 Bastiat Asks Are Politicians Greater Than Us? 105

Appendix #4 Bastiat Speaks of Legalized Plunder 107

Appendix #5 Government: Universal Physician? Unlimited Treasure? 108

Appendix #6 Money, Power, and Control 109

Appendix #7 – GDP per Capita Activity 114

Appendix #8 Brief Timeline of the Great Depression 124

Bibliography/Additional Reading 130

Glossary 131

About the Author 133

Preface

Economics gets a bad rap among so many, and yet as a long-time student and teacher of economics, I often wonder why. Maybe it's because most economic textbooks are so boring. In fact, I started this book after I looked unsuccessfully for an economics textbook that I could recommend for high schoolers. I found few options that didn't put me to sleep – and I like the topic! Thus began my desire to write an alternative economics textbook. Here it is, after more than two years, my contribution to teaching economics. I hope you and your students will soon find it as interesting a topic as I do.

Note: It is safe to say that all history and economics books are written from the point of view of the author(s) whether they state it or not. This book is written by a "classic liberal" – nowadays more often called a conservative, and that clearly shows throughout. If you are new to Austrian[1] economics, or confused by the difference between Austrian and Keynesian[2] economics, please read on.

---

[1] The school of economics I lean towards.
[2] The one most of the people in government today agree with.

How to Use This Book

I teach economics year after year, often to the same students. It is my opinion that it is too important a subject to be relegated to one semester during a student's high school years. But I am enough of a realist to realize that most people just want a tool to get through the required one semester. Hopefully this book will serve that purpose – as well as being a solid introduction to those who want to learn more.

This book is arranged in thirty-six lessons of different lengths. They can easily be completed in one semester by averaging two lessons/week, or you may want to spread the work out over a school year and do one lesson/week. By itself this textbook is meant to satisfy the half credit of economics that most high school students are required to have. You can easily turn it into an entire credit's worth of work if you desire by adding related readings from great resources such as the *Wall Street Journal* and FEE's monthly magazine, *Ideas on Liberty*. I give recommendations for some of those within the book and others can be found by searching on their websites. A student subscription to *Ideas on Liberty* is very inexpensive, and when I use those I generally find three to five articles in each one to have my students read.

For those who desire them, there are several review questions for each lesson. Most of them can be answered with the material covered in each lesson, though some do require the students to actually **think** about the material they have read.

If you need it, there is a Teacher Key available, also. It includes the answers to the mid-term and final exam included here, along with two classroom activities that you may find useful.

Introduction to Economics

So what is economics and why should we care? Economics is the study of the choices we make with scarce resources. By that definition we should **all** care!

If I had to choose one favorite economics book, it would be *Basic Economics* by Thomas Sowell.[3] If this book leaves you wanting to learn more, Sowell's is one of the first books I would recommend for additional reading. In his book Sowell asks the very important question, "Do we live in an 'Era of Scarcity' or an 'Era of Abundance?'"

While here in the United States we do live in an area that has more abundance than most of the rest of the world, and in an era that has more abundance than any before us, we still live with scarcities because there is not enough of anything to please everyone. Choices must always be made as to how to allocate and use the resources available.

If we all live with scarcity, then does that equal shortage? No! Scarcities cause individuals to make tradeoffs, but shortages are caused when the free market is tampered with, generally by the government; but more on that later. As Sowell said, *"The first lesson of economics is scarcity. There is never enough of anything to satisfy all those who want it. The first lesson of politics is to disregard the first lesson of economics."* [4]

Another great economist, Henry Hazlitt,[5] wrote shortly after World War II that *"Economics is haunted by more fallacies than any other study known to man."* Our goal in the next thirty-six lessons is to dispel some of those fallacies and hopefully make Economics more understandable in the process.

Microeconomics vs. Macroeconomics

Microeconomics focuses on the behavior of the consumer and individual businesses.

Macroeconomics is "the big picture" – or how things look at the national or world-wide level. Our focus here will be on some of both.

---

[3] Sowell is a 20th & 21st century American economist.
[4] As you go through the lessons, you will see how much economics politicians routinely try to ignore.
[5] Hazlitt was a 20th century American economist.

Lesson One - The Law of Unintended Consequences

I had planned to start with a lesson on price, supply and demand, since those are among the basic principles that must be understood in order to fully grasp other economic concepts. But I realized that possibly even more foundational is the idea of Unintended Consequences – and what Frederick Bastiat[6] once described as Seen and Not Seen.

Frederick Bastiat

In politics, too many economic decisions are made based on the short term gains they seem to bring and by looking at what they will do for a small group of people. It is important that we look beyond the short term and ask, as Sowell does in his book, *Applied Economics*, "And then what will happen?" And that we keep asking that question until we more clearly see the unintended consequences – what will happen as a result of the policy that may not have been intended [or planned]. Bastiat explained it well in one of his economic essays, *"In the economic sphere an act produces not only one effect, but a series of effects. Of these effects, the first alone is immediate; it appears simultaneously with its cause; it is seen. The other effects emerge only subsequently; they are not seen; we are fortunate if we foresee them."*

An example of unintended consequences was the recent "Cash for Clunkers" plan. The idea was to incentivize people to replace their older vehicles with new, better-gas mileage vehicles. But the consequence of the plan (besides costing taxpayers quite a bit of money) was to decrease the supply of used vehicles available for sale, causing their prices to rise and hurting the very people the program claimed to aid – those in the lower income brackets. With all that it only accomplished a slight increase in average gas mileage across the nation.

---

[6] Bastiat was a French economist in the mid-19th century.

As we try to build a foundation of clear economic thinking in this book, there are concepts we must constantly come back to, including: What are the unintended consequences of this policy? What will happen next? What will not be seen? Only then can we truly grasp the economic realities that we encounter. As we continue with our lessons we will see the dangers of ignoring Bastiat's warning.

Bastiat's Parable of the Broken Window

Bastiat told a parable of a shopkeeper who had a window broken by a vandal. Bastiat reasoned correctly that if the shopkeeper spent six francs to replace the broken window, society was not better off as a whole because of his six franc expenditure, because that expenditure would come at the loss of a different six franc purchase. Also leaving the shopkeeper worse off than he was before the window was broken because of the alternative purchase he is now not making. Bastiat concluded his parable, *"Society loses the value of things which are uselessly destroyed, and we must assent to a maxim which will make the hair of protectionists stand on end – To break, to spoil, to waste, is not to encourage national labour, or more briefly, 'destruction is not profit.'"*

Bastiat looked beyond the immediate results of a policy and saw the unintended consequences that were sure to follow. Watch for the seen and unseen in the economic conversations around you – and particularly in the speeches of politicians.

Lesson Two – The Role of Prices

We often hear of the connection between supply and demand – if demand for a product goes up, supply will usually increase as well. For instance, in the hot weather the demand for coolers increases and producers try to meet that demand by increasing their supply. And if the demand drops, supplies will generally follow. (When a certain toy starts to lose popularity, producers drop their production, and therefore their supplies, as soon as they realize.)

That is typically the case, and we will come back to those ideas often. But most economic concepts can also be visualized as the relationship between the three factors of price, supply, and demand. We can show this relationship with a simple triangle, with price on top.

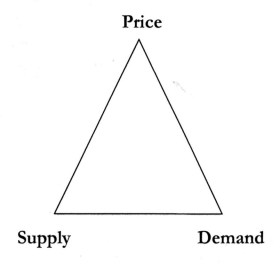

Price is the key to the triad. It communicates to all involved in that particular market: If prices go down, demand generally goes up. This is the consumers' response. (As is often witnessed when a business is running a big sale.) But if prices go down, supply will generally go down, also. (In response to these lower prices, it is unlikely that new businesses will rush to enter the market.) This is the producers' response.

All three of these, prices, supply, and demand work well together in a free market. Left alone they generally affect a market in the following manner: If demand goes up, price goes up, and then more suppliers can afford to get in the business. (Again, see the results when a certain toy gains popularity– more businesses may try to get in on the production or distribution of that toy while the prices are up.)

But if demand goes down, the price drops and "marginal producers"[7] are driven out of the market. As long as government doesn't interfere, supply, demand, and price will continue to regulate each other this way.

This textbook will not have as many graphs, charts, and numbers as most economics textbooks, but there are a few basic ones you should at least be aware of. Don't stress if the charts don't make total sense to you – they are here merely as an introduction.

"Law of Demand" – As the price of a good goes down, the demand tends to go up:

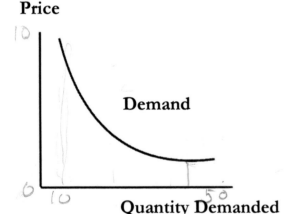

"Law of Supply" – As the price of a good goes up, the quantity supplied tends to go up:

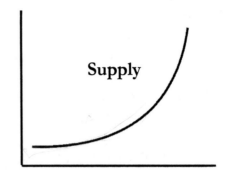

"Equilibrium" – The price and quantity at which the supply and demand curves intersect is the equilibrium price. When the price goes below that, more of the good is likely to be demanded than is likely to be supplied, causing a shortage. Likewise, we see a surplus if the price is held above the equilibrium price.

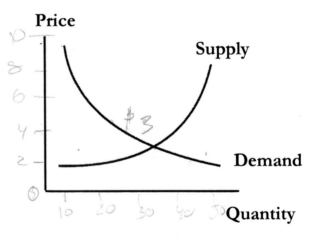

---

[7] Marginal producers are those who have higher costs and lower profits.

"Time is Money"

Here is another economic triad. In this one, the three concepts are in tension against each other. We generally have to choose which one (or two) we are willing to sacrifice in order to maximize the other(s). For instance, if we want something quickly (less time), we will generally have to give up quality, or pay a higher price. Or if we want higher quality, it will come at a higher price and/or with a larger commitment of time.

Keep both of these triads in mind in future lessons and as you consider the economic issues around you – price, supply, and demand and time, price, and quality. In addition to the twin ideas of unintended consequences and seen and unseen, these are foundational to the lessons that will come.

Lesson Three – Understanding Needs, Wants, and Incentives

Goods are useful things that satisfy our needs and wants. Our needs are those things we must have for survival – arguably food, shelter, and clothes. Our wants come into play when we want specific goods to satisfy those needs, or when we go beyond those basic needs.

Carl Menger[8] explained it well: *"Needs arise from our drives and the drives are imbedded in our nature. An imperfect satisfaction of needs leads to the stunting of our nature. Failure to satisfy them brings about our destruction. But to satisfy our needs is to live and prosper."* You notice he does not say that failure to satisfy our wants brings our destruction – those will never be truly satisfied. Menger went on to say, *"Wherever we turn among civilized peoples we find a system of large-scale advance provision for the satisfaction of human needs."*

Hopefully you will see through future lessons that the free market is best suited to provide those provisions.

Since economics is a science of choices, incentives are another fundamental concept of economics. People react to incentives and disincentives. If we incentivize them to do something, we shouldn't act surprised when they do it!

I like Lawrence W. Reed's[9] comment on incentives. *"Incentive – nothing less than the interest one has in his own improvement – will mold the future just as surely as it shaped the past."*

Corollary: If incentives change, choices will change.

Example: When prices go up, we are incentivized to conserve, just as when prices go down, we are incentivized to use more (spend more) of something. This is, of course, tied to how elastic our demand for that particular item is (which we will explain in the next lesson).

---

[8] Carl Menger was a 19th and 20th century economist who is credited with founding the Austrian School of economics.

[9] Lawrence W. Reed is a 20th and 21st century American economist.

Lesson Four - Elasticity of Demand

Is there a fixed supply of most things? No, as we saw earlier, supply can generally increase to help meet growing demand. (It's only a question of how quickly and at what price!)

Is there a fixed demand for most things? No, not for most things. We call how fixed the demand is the elasticity of demand. This is one of many places that textbooks often throw in graphs and numbers (and I will follow that trend – but only with four simple graphs). But the important part of the concept is "How much will the demand change in relation to changing prices?" Something that is quite inelastic will maintain similar demand curves across many price changes. On the other hand, demand for something that is quite elastic will change dramatically with drastic price changes. (If the demand is fairly elastic we usually figure out quickly that we can "live without" that favorite brand at double or triple the price.)

An example of a fairly inelastic demand for most of us is gasoline, at least in the short term. We have to have a certain amount of it each week to get to work and to meet our other obligations, and within a fairly wide range of prices, we will buy at least that much.

Something that is highly elastic might be our demand for a certain cut of meat. We might prefer flank steak for our barbeque, but we can substitute a different kind of beef, or even chicken. So if the price of flank steak goes up significantly, we will make a substitution.

Few purchases fall at either extreme; most fall somewhere near one of the middle two. Influences on elasticity can include: how important the item is to us, how frequent (or seldom) it is purchased, and what types of substitutes exist for it.

Here are four simple elasticity graphs to give you an idea.[10]

First: Totally Inelastic (No change in demand, regardless of price)

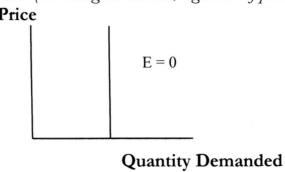

Second: Some Change

Third: More Change

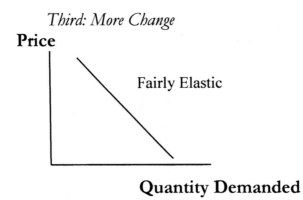

---

[10] I've shown the graphs with straight lines for simplicity's sake, but lines of elasticity are seldom completely linear.

Fourth: Totally Elastic (Only desired at one price)

Price

E = infinite

Quantity Demanded

Lesson Five – Entrepreneurs and Opportunity Cost

Entrepreneurs could be referred to as the engines of society. They are generally the ones that take the risks and work to bring about positive changes through their innovation and hard work. They don't take risks for the fun of it – they are trying to make a profit in the process. While they wait to (hopefully) make that profit, their workers continue to get paid.

Henry Ford and his contribution to the auto industry and Steve Jobs and his contribution to the personal computer industry are two examples of well-known entrepreneurs.

Ford's contributions were increased by his use of the assembly line and standardization; through those he revolutionized auto production.

1912 Roadster

Another important concept in economics that involves entrepreneurs is opportunity cost. (Everyone experiences opportunity cost when they are making decisions that involve how they spend their time and money, but it may be easier to see it with the entrepreneurs.)

Opportunity cost is really about "the next best option." An example of opportunity cost is what an entrepreneur would most likely have done with his time and money had he not started his business. (What would he have been getting paid if he were managing an existing business, for example is the opportunity cost of starting a business instead of receiving a regular salary; what interest could he have earned on his money if he had invested it in the bank instead of his business is also an opportunity cost.)

I like Hazlitt's explanation of Opportunity Cost: *"Everything, in short, is produced at the expense of foregoing something else. Costs of production themselves, in fact, might be defined as the things that are given up (the leisure and pleasures, the raw materials with alternative potential uses) in order to create the thing that is made."*

Lesson Six - The Constitution and Economics

– uTUBE video

Wait, you might be saying, this is a book on Economics, not Government! But, as we will see throughout the book, the two topics can hardly be separated. While our country does go back a few years before our Constitution (1776 versus 1787), the Constitution is the foundation of our current government system. As such, it can hardly be ignored when we are looking at the economic situation of our country. It also deals with many of the macroeconomic issues that will come up throughout the study so it is a good place to start.

You probably already know that the Constitution is divided into seven sections (called Articles). We will look briefly now at the portions of those articles that deal with economic principles. You may be surprised at what the Constitution does and does not say about economics.

Starting with the Preamble we see the first references to economic principles in the Constitution:

Preamble: *We the People of the United States, in order to form a more perfect Union, establish Justice, insure domestic Tranquility, provide for the common Defense, promote the general Welfare, and secure the Blessings of Liberty to ourselves and our Posterity, do ordain and establish this Constitution for the United States of America.*

The **Preamble** gives us the premise behind our government: insuring domestic tranquility (peace), providing defense, and promoting the general welfare. Do you see how peace and defense are meant to be done by the government – but the general welfare is merely promoted?

In **Article 1** the founders laid out the requirements and limitations of the Legislative Branch. In the midst of discussing who is eligible to be representatives, there is the first reference to taxes (though you will notice they differ significantly from the taxes we think of today):

Section 2. *...Representatives and direct Taxes shall be apportioned among the several States which may be included within* *this Union, according to their respective Numbers...*

In **Article 1, Section 7** economics comes up again in reference to types of bills:

Section. 7. *All Bills for raising Revenue shall originate in the House of Representatives; but the Senate may propose or concur with Amendments as on other Bills.*

In **Article 1, Section 8**, the real economic discussion begins as the Constitution lays out what the responsibilities of Congress were to be. You can highlight or underline the various economic principles you find in the remaining sections of the Constitution. When you are finished, consider whether this is more or less than what you expected to find:

Article 1, Section. 8. *The Congress shall have Power To lay and collect Taxes, Duties, Imposts and Excises, to pay the Debts and provide for the common Defense and general Welfare of the United States; but all Duties, Imposts and Excises shall be uniform throughout the United States;*

- *To borrow Money on the credit of the United States;*
- *To regulate Commerce with foreign Nations, and among the several States, and with the Indian Tribes;*
- *To establish an uniform Rule of Naturalization, and uniform Laws on the subject of Bankruptcies throughout the United States;*
- *To coin Money, regulate the Value thereof, and of foreign Coin, and fix the Standard of Weights and Measures;*
- *To provide for the Punishment of counterfeiting the Securities and current Coin of the United States;*
- *To establish Post Offices and post Roads;*
- *To promote the Progress of Science and useful Arts, by securing for limited Times to Authors and Inventors the exclusive Right to their respective Writings and Discoveries;*
- *To constitute Tribunals inferior to the supreme Court;*
- *To define and punish Piracies and Felonies committed on the high Seas, and Offences against the Law of Nations;*
- *To declare War, grant Letters of Marque and Reprisal, and make Rules concerning Captures on Land and Water;*
- *To raise and support Armies, but no Appropriation of Money to that Use shall be for a longer Term than two Years;*
- *To provide and maintain a Navy;*
- *To make Rules for the Government and Regulation of the land and naval Forces;*
- *To provide for calling forth the Militia to execute the Laws of the Union,*

- suppress Insurrections and repel Invasions;
- To provide for organizing, arming, and disciplining, the Militia, and for governing such Part of them as may be employed in the Service of the United States, reserving to the States respectively, the Appointment of the Officers, and the Authority of training the Militia according to the discipline prescribed by Congress;
- To exercise exclusive Legislation in all Cases whatsoever, over such District (not exceeding ten Miles square) as may, by Cession of particular States, and the Acceptance of Congress, become the Seat of the Government of the United States, and to exercise like Authority over all Places purchased by the Consent of the Legislature of the State in which the Same shall be, for the Erection of Forts, Magazines, Arsenals, dock-Yards, and other needful Buildings;--And
- To make all Laws which shall be necessary and proper for carrying into Execution the foregoing Powers, and all other Powers vested by this Constitution in the Government of the United States, or in any Department or Officer thereof.

Article 1, Section. 9. ...*No Capitation, or other direct, Tax shall be laid, unless in Proportion to the Census or enumeration herein before directed to be taken.*

- No Tax or Duty shall be laid on Articles exported from any State.
- No Preference shall be given by any Regulation of Commerce or Revenue to the Ports of one State over those of another; nor shall Vessels bound to, or from, one State, be obliged to enter, clear, or pay Duties in another.
- No Money shall be drawn from the Treasury, but in Consequence of Appropriations made by Law; and a regular Statement and Account of the Receipts and Expenditures of all public Money shall be published from time to time....

Article 1, Section. 10. *No State shall enter into any Treaty, Alliance, or Confederation; grant Letters of Marque and Reprisal; coin Money; emit Bills of Credit; make any Thing but gold and silver Coin a Tender in Payment of Debts; pass any Bill of Attainder, ex post facto Law, or Law impairing the Obligation of Contracts, or grant any Title of Nobility.*

- No State shall, without the Consent of the Congress, lay any Imposts or Duties on Imports or Exports, except what may be absolutely necessary for executing it's inspection Laws: and the net Produce of all Duties and Imposts, laid by any State on Imports or Exports, shall be for the Use of the Treasury of the United States; and all such Laws shall be subject to the Revision and Controul of the Congress.
- No State shall, without the Consent of Congress, lay any Duty of Tonnage,

keep Troops, or Ships of War in time of Peace, enter into any Agreement or Compact with another State, or with a foreign Power, or engage in War, unless actually invaded, or in such imminent Danger as will not admit of delay.

Article 2. Deals with the Executive Department (the President).

Article 3. Deals with the Judicial Department (the Supreme Court).

Article 4. Deals with citizenship and the relationship between states.

Article 5. Deals with the Amendment process of the Constitution.

In **Article 6** we see a couple more important economic references, and the laying down of the Constitution as the supreme law of the land: *All Debts contracted and Engagements entered into, before the Adoption of this Constitution, shall be as valid against the United States under this Constitution, as under the Confederation.*

This Constitution, and the Laws of the United States which shall be made in Pursuance thereof; and all Treaties made, or which shall be made, under the Authority of the United States, shall be the supreme Law of the Land; and the Judges in every State shall be bound thereby, any Thing in the Constitution or Laws of any State to the Contrary notwithstanding…

With **Article 7** giving the ratification process of the Constitution, the original document ended.

A few more economic concepts show up in some of the Amendments to the Constitution. The Fifth Amendment is where the concept of "Eminent Domain"[11] is introduced – with its limitations: **Amendment 5:** *"…nor shall any person…be deprived of life, liberty, or property, without due process of law; nor shall private property be taken for public use, without just compensation."*

Amendment 8: *"Excessive bail shall not be required, nor excessive fines imposed, nor cruel and unusual punishments inflicted."*

While the Tenth Amendment is not overtly economic, it would be safe to say that there are economic overtones to it:

---

[11] Eminent Domain is the idea that the government can require a private individual to sell their property because the government has need of it. There is an www.izzit.org DVD dealing with this important concept: *Unintended Consequences: Eminent Domain* (dealing with the Kelo case in New London, CT).

Amendment 10: *"The powers not delegated to the United States by the Constitution, nor prohibited by it to the States, are reserved to the States respectively, or to the people."*

In the Fourteenth Amendment, aspects of the Fifth Amendment were applied to the states: **Amendment 14** (ratified in 1868*)*: *"…No State shall make or enforce any law which shall abridge the privileges or immunities of citizens of the United States; nor shall any State deprive any person of life, liberty, or property, without due process of law; nor deny to any person within its jurisdiction the equal protection of the laws."*

In 1913, income taxes became a part of American life: **Amendment 16**: *"The Congress shall have power to lay and collect taxes on incomes, from whatever source derived, without apportionment among the several States, and without regard to any census or enumeration."*

In 1919 the Constitution was amended to prohibit the sale of alcohol in the United States: **Amendment 18:** *"After one year from the ratification of this article the manufacture, sale, or transportation of intoxicating liquors within, the importation thereof into, or the exportation thereof from the United States and all territory subject to the jurisdiction thereof for beverage purposes is hereby prohibited."* (But, of course, in 1933, that amendment was repealed – the only amendment to be repealed to date.)

How was your economic search through the U.S. Constitution?

Lesson Seven – Important Economic Philosophies

As with all areas of history, having the context is extremely important. Our country and our constitution didn't spring from thin air, and neither did our economic way of thinking.

During the early days of the American colonies, the popular economic philosophy in Europe was **mercantilism** – the belief that a state must accumulate as much gold and silver as possible in order to be wealthy. The mercantilism philosophy encouraged exports and discouraged imports, not understanding the important connection between those.

Adam Smith

In 1759, Adam Smith, a Scottish professor of logic and philosophy, published *The Theory of Moral Sentiments*, where he first used the term the **"invisible hand"** to explain his belief that the marketplace would self-regulate, in spite of the profit motives of the individual sellers, with no overarching, controlling entity. He believed that **labor** was the source of a nation's wealth, not the quantity of gold or silver it possessed.

In the 1750's the Frenchman Vincent de Gournay popularized the slogan **"laissez faire"** – meaning "let it be" or "leave it alone." His original slogan was actually "Laissez faire et laissez passer, le monde va de lui meme!" – *"Let do and let pass, the world goes on by itself."*

Gournay influenced the **physiocrats** - a group of French scholars and merchants in the mid to late 18th century who criticized the mercantile system. These physiocrats argued for limited government interference, and for the need to measure a society's wealth based on its **land**, not its manufacturing. The physiocrats believed in individual liberty and property rights and believed that the mercantilist system led to excessive regulations. They also encouraged governments to abolish barriers against trade.

From 1763 to 1766 Adam Smith travelled from Scotland to Europe as a tutor. His travels put him in contact with the French physiocrats. That contact influenced his next work, *The Wealth of Nations*, where he spoke again of the influence of an "invisible hand." When *The Wealth of Nations* was first published in 1776, it quickly became a fundamental work in classic economics. In addition to expanding on his idea of the "invisible hand," it also covered division of labor, the origin and use of money, wages, interest rates and more.

Many of the founders of our country were influenced by Smith's work, though Alexander Hamilton, the first Treasury Secretary of the United States, was one of those who believed in high tariffs and a national bank.

Karl Marx

In the late 19th century Karl Marx[12] emphasized labor to the point that he believed class struggle was a good thing, believing workers should overthrow the capitalists who were "taking advantage of them."

John Maynard Keynes

Fast forward to the early 20th century and we encounter a British economist, John Maynard Keynes, who pioneered a new philosophy that has come to be known as **Keynesian** economics. In the midst of the Great Depression Keynes argued for more government intervention, rather than less. Since he believed that too little demand caused unemployment he taught that government budget deficits would somehow help restore full employment and lift the country out of the Depression. The effects of his philosophy are being felt today.

In the mid-20th century Ludwig von Mises, an Austrian economist would argue again for laissez-faire government and free markets. He is

---

[12] Karl Marx was a 19th century German economist who rejected Adam Smith's ideas and spoke positively of "communal property" rather than private property.

credited with further development of the Austrian school of economic thought (founded previously by Carl Menger). Followers of the Austrian School of thought included Friedrich Hayek and Henry Hazlitt.

The Invisible Hand

As we said earlier, the "invisible hand" was Smith's way of explaining that the marketplace would self-regulate, in spite of the profit motives of individual sellers.[13]

In his first book, *The Theory of Moral Sentiments*, Smith wrote, *"The proud and unfeeling landlord views his extensive fields, and without a thought for the wants of his brethren, in imagination consumes himself the whole harvest...The rich...are led by an invisible hand to make nearly the same distribution of the necessaries of life, which would have been made, had the earth been divided into equal portions among all its inhabitants, and thus without intending it, without knowing it, advance the interest of the society..."*

In his second book, the *Wealth of Nations*, Smith wrote, *"Every individual...neither intends to promote the public interest, nor knows how much he is promoting it...By directing that industry in such a manner as its produce may be of the greatest value, he intends only his own gain, and he is in this, as in many other cases, led by an invisible hand to promote an end which was no part of his intention...By pursuing his own interest he frequently promotes that of the society more effectually than when he really intends to promote it."*

Most classical economists agree with Smith's idea of "the invisible hand" – that free markets can self-regulate better than they can be regulated through any government-mandated regulations.

---

[13] For a great article with more about the importance of this concept today, see the article on www.FEE.org, "Adam Smith and the Invisible Hand."

Lesson Eight – Money, Money, Money

Barter involves direct exchange between buyer and seller, but that can make transactions more complicated. For instance, if you wanted to buy my chicken, but I didn't want your vegetables, I wanted someone else's cloth, things got difficult. The limitations of barter led people to indirect exchanges, which led people to the need for some type of money as a medium of exchange.

Bastiat explained the medium of money well: *"Properly speaking, exchange is the reciprocity of services. The parties say between themselves 'Give me this and I will give you that;' or 'Do this for me and I will do that for you.'"* As we stated, Bastiat also explained, *"In reality, services are scarcely ever exchanged directly. There is a medium, which is termed money."* Therefore money facilitates trade, by making our transactions more efficient.

Bastiat then went on to quote another French economist, Jean-Baptiste Say, who had said, *"Since the introduction of money, every exchange is resolved into two elements, sale and purchase. It is the reunion of these two elements which render the exchange complete."* Every exchange, every transaction, consists of a buyer and a seller.

Money has been many things over the years and around the world – including sea shells, salt, and gold. To be a good medium for money, something generally needs to be transportable, divisible, durable, and convenient, and gold and silver work well for those.

In the late Middle Ages, when gold started being accepted as a universal means of trading, goldsmiths started storing larger and larger quantities of gold for individuals. In time these goldsmiths became the first banks. With banks eventually came the idea of not only storing the money, but also loaning that money, and in time banks learned that they could safely loan out a certain percentage of their stores at a time. (In our country the Federal Reserve dictates to banks how much of a percentage they must keep in reserve.)

Obviously, if banks are loaning some of the money to others and suddenly everyone wants their money back out at the same time, there is going to be a problem – a "run on the banks"! For an easy to understand look at a run on the banks see the scenes in *Mary Poppins* and *It's A wonderful Life* (both are available on YouTube).

When the United States first started using paper money we were on a gold standard (meaning the money was backed by a certain amount of gold). You may want to go back to Lesson 6 and review what Article 1, Sections 8 and 10 say about the United States and money.

In 1933 President Franklin D. Roosevelt started the process of replacing the gold based money with fiat money.[14] President Richard Nixon completed the process in 1971.

While it might be argued that a gold standard is not absolutely critical for a country's economic health, Mises made this important point about it: *"The gold standard has one tremendous virtue: the quantity of money under the gold standard is independent of the policies of governments and political parties…It is a form of protection against spendthrift governments…Under a gold standard, sound government has a much better chance."* Without a gold standard, the purchasing power of money is more easily manipulated, often by inflationary measures that cause a decrease in the standard of living, especially of those who are on a fixed income.

Central Banks

A whole study could be done on the role of central banks in the United States, but that goes beyond this introductory book. It will suffice here just to mention their existence in American history: The first central bank was called the First Bank of the United States and it was in place from 1792 – 1812; the Second Bank of the United States was in place from 1816 – 1836. The third central bank is the Federal Reserve, which has been with us since 1913. Much more could be said about central banks in general and the Federal Reserve in particular, but again, that's beyond what we will address here. To find good information on it from an Austrian perspective, type Federal Reserve into the search box of Mises.org.

---

[14] Money that is only "valuable" because the government has declared it so – since it is not backed by gold, silver, or any other valuable asset.

Lesson Nine – Standard of Living

It should be understood that money and wealth are not the same thing; especially now that our money has become a representative of something valuable and has no value in and of itself. When the government interferes with the supply of money, the amount of the money we possess may increase dramatically, but if what we can purchase with that money has decreased rather than increased, our wealth has not increased, even if our money supply has. (We will talk more about inflation in Lesson Thirty-Five.)

As Fred Schnaubelt explained in his book, *Romancing the Voters:* "A standard of living depends upon how many hours of work it takes to buy food, clothing, shelter, etc., --- how productive you are."

Decades earlier Mises spoke passionately about what the standard of living really means when he delivered a series of economic talks in Argentina:

I fully agree with the ultimate goal of raising the standard of living everywhere. But I disagree about the measures to be adapted in obtaining this goal…Not protection, not government interference, not socialism, and certainly not the violence of the labor unions…An increase in real wages, results not only in an increase in population, it results also, and first of all, in an improvement in the average standard of living…this higher standard of living depends on the supply of capital.

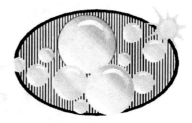

For a great visual of the changing standards of living throughout the world over the last two hundred years, google "Hans Rosling, 200 Countries, 200 years." In four minutes Rosling shows you changing standards of living in an amazing way.

The way we compute a country's wealth is through their GDP – gross domestic product (considered the total market value of all final goods produced in a country). While it is not a perfect measure, it does give us a point of comparison for a country from one year to another, or from one country to another.

Another imperfect, but useful, tool is GDP per capita – the average gross domestic product per individual in a country. Again, this can be a very useful tool in making comparisons. **Appendix #7** includes a multi-page chart listing countries from highest to lowest GDP per capita and a graph you can complete with the GDP per capita of ten of the countries of your choice. Before you look at the chart, where do you think your country will be on the list?

Obviously a figure like GDP per capita is distorted for countries where there are very rich people and very poor people. But it still gives a great starting point for comparisons between different countries (since total GDP would not account for population differences).

Do Appendix #7 for Monday w/ Joe and questions in Back for lesson 7

Lesson Ten – Greed, Self-Interest, and Profit

Do we believe Milton Friedman's[15] quote: *"Greed is not a bad thing. Self interest is not a bad thing."* Or does that strike a negative chord with us? From a character standpoint we think of greed and self-interest as negative attributes. We don't want to be thought of as greedy, and we certainly don't want to be told we think only of ourselves! But in the world of business, greed and self-interest are not quite the same thing. But wait, you may be thinking, I've been hearing about greedy businessmen for years. Let's step back and look at these concepts realistically.

Over two hundred years ago Adam Smith wrote, *"It is not from the benevolence of the butcher, the brewer, or the baker, that we expect our dinner, but from their regard to their own self-interest. We address ourselves, not to their humanity, but to their self-love, and never talk to them of our own necessities, but of their advantages."*

Just as Adam Smith's baker and butcher have their own self-interests in mind, so do businesses. That is not evil, it is logical. So then why is making a profit so often demonized in the media or by politicians? Do we really expect companies to stay in business without making a profit?

In the Soviet Union they simply outlawed profits. But what was the result? Massive shortages of critical consumer goods – that could not be bought at any price.

Additionally, only the market, through profits and losses, can efficiently lead a company to pursue innovation. When losses or insufficient profits occur, a company is motivated to pursue alternative processes or to devote the labor and capital to something else altogether.

In short, profits are an important part of the market process![16]

---

[15] 20th/21st century American economist; Friedman was awarded the 1976 Nobel Prize in Economics.

[16] For more on this important topic, see the Freeman article, "What is Profit?" available on their website, www.fee.org.

Lesson Eleven – Division of Labor

In order for a society to increase the standard or living of its members (which goes hand in hand with it moving from primitive to more industrialized), the division of labor is necessary. Division of labor is the concept of individuals specializing in different tasks (therefore increasing efficiency and productivity). Division of Labor is more efficient because it promotes automation; people gravitate towards tasks they are good at; and switching between tasks wastes time. When individuals produce more than they will personally consume they move towards specialization and division of labor. Instead of being self-sufficient, they will only produce a portion of what they will consume, and enter into transactions with other individuals to fulfill their other needs and wants.

Only once we have started specializing can we become more efficient in production and start increasing capital. Adam Smith wrote much in *The Wealth of Nations* on the subject of the division of labor. I have included a larger section of that chapter as **Appendix #1,** but here have only included a small section of it:

"The greatest improvements in the productive powers of labour, and the greater part of the skill, dexterity, and judgment…seem to have been the effects of the division of labour….The division of labour…occasions, in every art, a proportionable increase of the productive powers of labour. The separation of different trades and employments from one another, seems to have taken place in consequence of this advantage…The labour, too, which is necessary to produce any one complete manufacture, is almost always divided among a great number of hands…

"It is the great multiplication of the productions of all the different arts, in consequence of the division of labour, which occasions, in a well-governed society, that universal opulence which extends itself to the lowest ranks of the people. Every workman has a great quantity of his own work to dispose of beyond what he himself has occasion for; and every other workman being exactly in the same situation, he is enabled

to exchange a great quantity of his own goods for a great quantity or, what comes to the same thing, for the price of a great quantity of theirs. He supplies them abundantly with what they have occasion for, and they accommodate him as amply with what he has occasion for, and a general plenty diffuses itself through all the different ranks of the society."

Menger didn't give division of labor quite as much credit for improving society as Smith did: *"Correctly it should be regarded only as one factor among the great influences that lead mankind from barbarism and misery to civilization and wealth."*

But Menger also said, *"Nothing is more certain than that the degree of economic progress of mankind will still...be commensurate with the degree of human knowledge."*

So while division of labor may not be the only thing a society needs to improve its overall condition, the simple act of division of labor does lead to more productivity, and contributes to moving a society to a higher standard of living.

Lesson Twelve – The Evils of Machinery?

Are machines responsible for increasing our unemployment and our woes? Or are they a blessing? Do they somehow improve our lives as individuals and yet still hamper society as a whole? Over 150 years ago Bastiat was already arguing that *"To curse machines is to curse the spirit of humanity!"*

Even before then, Adam Smith made the following observation about machines: *"I shall only observe, therefore, that the invention of all those machines by which labour is so much facilitated and abridged, seems to have been originally owing to the division of labour...A great part of the machines made use of in those manufactures in which labour is most subdivided, were originally the invention of common workmen, who, being each of them employed in some very simple operation, naturally turned their thoughts towards finding out easier and readier methods of performing it."*

As Smith and Bastiat would both have agreed, machines can, and generally are, used to improve our lives. Yet they are still viewed with suspicion by so many. But do we really want to live our lives without the comforts that machines have enabled us to have? Or the life-saving technologies that have been developed as a result?

What are the arguments against them? During the Industrial Revolution and many times since, the concern has been expressed that machines would displace workers. Sometimes concerns escalated to riots and then to violence. For example – in England in the 1860's handicraft workers worried about their jobs destroyed over 1000 new stocking frames during a riot and threatened the inventors. There was some validity to their concerns – in the short run. But in the long run more workers were employed in the industry than had been before the frames came along – and the workers were more productive.

Earlier in the mid-18th century the same phenomenon had happened in the textile industry. Before the invention of Arkwright's[17] cotton-spinning machinery less than 8,000 workers were employed in England in the production of cotton textiles. Less than three decades later there

---

[17] Sir Richard Arkwright, an English entrepreneur who invented machinery that improved spinning operations.

were more than 300,000 such workers.[18]

In 1932, during the Depression, machines were blamed again for rising unemployment – this time by a group calling themselves "Technocrats." It would be years before the errors behind their claims would be corrected. Even so, in 1945, still continuing that myth, President Roosevelt's wife wrote, *"We have reached a point today where labor-saving devices are good only when they do not throw the worker out of his job."*

A thinking person should stop and ask, how far back would Mrs. Roosevelt have us go – back to before refrigerators, so the ice man still has a job, or before cars so that horse and carriages could be rehired, or before electric lights so that lamplighters could again have jobs? With each of these labor-saving devices has come a higher standard of living – and most of us do not want to return to the pre-industrialized days that did not include them.

So what is the truth when manufacturers replace workers with machines? Even when the number of employees does go down – it is not a loss for society. If the manufacturer is now making higher profits (which would generally be the reason for adding machinery), he will expand his operation, invest his extra profit, or spend his extra money (or some combination). All three of those options will make society better off.

If his product goes down in price because of the increased productivity, more people will be able to buy it, and the people buying it will have money left over to spend on something else! So the actual result of increased machinery is increased productivity – which raises the standard of living (just as the division of labor did, that we discussed earlier).

It is safe to say that increased productivity is required to raise a society's standard of living – productivity that increases with standardization, division of labor, and machinery. So instead of seeing them as the enemies of progress, new machines should be seen as a benefit to both those who are on the production side and those who are on the consumption side.

---

[18] Henry Hazlitt explains this well in his chapter on "The Curse of Machinery" in his book *Economics in One Lesson*.

Lesson Thirteen – Markets

Markets consist of transactions between multiple buyers and sellers, for a variety of goods (the physical items that are bought and sold) and services (the intangible actions that are performed). Those goods and services are purchased to satisfy perceived needs and wants.

These are the three steps that a good must go through along its path to market:

1. It must be supplied through some sort of **production**.
2. It must make it from the supplier to the consumer through some sort of **distribution** (this may be a simple step or a more complicated one).
3. Then it is **"consumed"** by the demander. Obviously not all items are consumed in the sense of being used up (dining room furniture versus dinner, for instance), but it is all used by the Consumer in some way.

Obviously this is an over-simplification, but it gives you an idea of the three primary stages of a product: Production, Distribution, and Consumption.

Of course, goods are not produced from thin air. A producer must use some combination of natural resources,[19] labor, and capital[20] to produce goods.

The other distinction we can make is between consumer goods and capital goods. Consumer goods are those things that are purchased by individuals to fulfill their personal wants or needs. Capital goods[21] (sometimes called production goods) are the man-made tools and equipment used by businesses to make consumer goods. Capital goods are one of the areas many businesses have to make sizeable investments in on the path to production.

---

[19] Natural resources include land, water, minerals, and other such resources.
[20] Capital is the wealth used in production.

[21] Capital goods are produced with some combination of other goods and labor, and have value based on their production capabilities.

Lesson Fourteen – Capital and Capital Goods

Sometimes the terms "capital" and "capital goods" are used interchangeably. Capital, broadly speaking, equals wealth used in the process of production. Some economic books will speak of different types of capital – "financial capital," or money; "physical capital," the roads and factories used in production; "natural capital," as the natural world; etc. Let's look at what four different economists had to say about capital over the centuries.

In the 18th century, Adam Smith used the term over 400 times in *The Wealth of Nations*. Here's what he had to say about it in one place:

"There are two different ways in which a capital may be employed so as to yield a revenue or profit to its employer. First, it may be employed in raising, manufacturing, or purchasing goods, and selling them again with a profit. The capital employed in this manner yields no revenue or profit to its employer, while it either remains in his possession, or continues in the same shape.

The goods of the merchant yield him no revenue or profit till he sells them for money, and the money yields him as little till it is again exchanged for goods. His capital is continually going from him in one shape, and returning to him in another; and it is only by means of such circulation, or successive changes, that it can yield him any profit. Such capitals, therefore, may very properly be called circulating capitals.

Secondly, it may be employed in the improvement of land, in the purchase of useful machines and instruments of trade, or in such like things as yield a revenue or profit without changing masters, or circulating any further. Such capitals, therefore, may very properly be called fixed capitals. Different occupations require very different proportions between the fixed and circulating capitals employed in them."

In the 19th century, Bastiat also discussed capital:

"What is capital, then? It is composed of three things: first of the materials upon which men operate...wool, flax, leather, silk, wood, etc. Second, instruments which are used for working — tools, machines, ships, carriages, etc.

Third, provisions which are consumed during labour — victuals, stuffs, houses, etc. Without these things the labour of man would be unproductive and almost void; yet these very things have required much work, especially at first. This is the reason that so much value has been attached to the possession of them, and also that it is perfectly lawful to exchange and to sell them, to make a profit of them if used, to gain remuneration from them if lent."

Early in the 20th century Hazlitt added these words, *"Producers invest in new capital goods — that is they buy new and better and more ingenious tools — because these tools reduce cost of production."*

Later Mises said this of capital:

"The difference between the U.S. and other countries is not personal inferiority or ignorance. The difference is the supply of capital, the quantity of capital goods available. In other words, the amount of capital invested per unit of the population is greater in the so-called advanced nations than in the developing nations."

Clearly the capital on which capitalism is based is a positive thing, not a negative one!

Lesson Fifteen – Voluntary Exchanges and Free Trade

As we discussed earlier a free market scenario involves voluntary exchange – voluntary exchange between individuals who are making countless decisions based on their perceived needs, wants, and prices.

As Frederic Bastiat said over 150 years ago, *"When a man by his labour has made some useful thing – in other words, when he has created a value – it can only pass into the hands of another by one of the following modes – as a gift, by exchange, loan, or theft."*

The voluntary portion of exchange is important because otherwise, as Bastiat expounds on it: *"If it were to be asserted on principle, admitted in practice, or sanctioned by law, that every man has a right to the property of another…charity and gratitude would no longer be virtues. Besides, such a doctrine would suddenly and universally arrest labour and production…for who would work if there was no longer to be any connection between labour and the satisfying of our wants?…That which a man has produced, he may consume, exchange, or give."*

As we see, voluntary exchange, or free markets, are not a win-lose or lose-lose situation, they are a win-win situation. The exchange does not take place unless both parties consider themselves better off as a result. (An important concept to keep in mind when we discuss exports and imports later – both countries are better off in an import-export exchange.)

So, whether the trade is within our country, or around the world, it needs to be fully understood that free trade is voluntary trade, as such, both the buyer and the seller must be happy for a transaction to take place. With complete choice (i.e. no government limits or other interference), free trade[22] is the best functioning and most equitable situation. As Mises once said, *"The capitalist system of production is an economic democracy in which every penny gives a right to vote. Consumers are the sovereign people."*

---

[22] See the www.Izzit.org DVD – Free Trade (for a comparison between the economic systems of Sweden, Hong Kong, and the U.S.)

Lesson Sixteen – Capitalism vs. Socialism/Communism

There are two different ways to look at how government should behave economically – should it be constrained (the capitalist, free market view) or unconstrained (the socialist view)? Most countries fall somewhere between the totally constrained and totally unconstrained and needless to say, the different types of government produce very different results.

Americans have not always practiced capitalism. The early Pilgrim settlers practiced a form of communism[23] from 1621 – 1623. It was a dismal failure, but just as John Smith had helped turn the Jamestown settlement around a few years earlier, William Bradford would help turn around the Plymouth settlement.[24]

Governor Bradford wrote of their experience in his book, *Of Plymouth Plantation*, "*The experience that was had in this common course and condition…was found to breed much confusion & discontent, and retard much employment that would have been to their benefit and comfort.*" (For more from this passage, see **Appendix #2** – *The Pilgrims Try Communism*.) Stop and Read p 104

Centuries later Karl Marx, believing that labor equaled value, coined the term "capitalism" – as a negative – to describe what he considered the worst of all economic systems, since he considered capitalism to be all about the capitalists, who he saw as stealing from laborers.

But Mises saw capitalism in a positive way. It *"describes clearly the source of the great social improvements brought about by capitalism. These improvements are the result of capital accumulation; they are based on the fact that people, as a rule, do not consume everything they have produced, that they save – and invest – a part of it."*

---

[23] Socialism generally refers to an economic system – while communism is both economic and political. (Communism is also thought of as an extreme version of socialism.)

[24] The izzit.org DVD, *Yours & Mine: The Lesson of 1623*, shows this problem in a goofy but effective way.

Not only is capitalism about improvements, it is about freedom – from the freedom to make choices in what we purchase to the freedom in where we work and to make our own mistakes. But in socialist societies, the government owns and controls the means of production, limiting its effective-ness. In a socialist, or command economy, the decisions are made by a relatively small group of politicians. See Bastiat's great thoughts on them in *Appendix #3 – Bastiat's Thoughts on "Are Politicians Greater Than Us?"*

Lesson Seventeen – Central Planning: Individual Knowledge vs. Collective Knowledge

In a socialized economy, the government is doing the planning – the "central planning." The government attempts to control production, distribution, and consumption (to at least some degree). Private Property almost (or completely) ceases to exist. Competition doesn't exist. In the extreme version, wages are fixed.

One of the results of central planning is that the government overrides the plans of private individuals and corporations.[25] When planning is left to the government, prices are set by the planners instead of being dictated by supply and demand.

This causes an inefficient use of resources and the predictable shortages and surpluses found throughout the USSR for years, and similar problems in other countries like India and China who have similarly tried "central planning."

In a free society planning is done by individuals. As we've said before, prices will fall and rise to signal needed changes in supply and demand to both consumers and producers. Since all things have a cost associated with them – central planning requires the cost to be paid by the collective, while the free market ensures that individuals pay the cost when they make their purchases. Which do you think works more effectively?

Fred Schnaubelt explained the difference between central planning and a free market system in his book, *Romancing the Voters*, *"The basic problem of every complex society is how to coordinate the economic activities of large numbers of people. When decisions number in the trillions every day, it takes the collective wisdom of the free market, the decisions of all the actors, to bring order out of chaos. By contrast, it is impossible for any government to collect all the pertinent data, sort it, correlate it, prioritize it, and act upon it in a timely or efficient manner.*

Consider how the free market brings affordable priced food to over 315 million Americans three times a day without any centralized, coercive direction of a government agency, just the voluntary

---

[25] Thomas Sowell speaks of this in his book, *Applied Economics*.

cooperation among farmers, distributors, warehousemen, groceries, restaurants, and consumers all acting in their own 'self-interest.'" This is Smith's "invisible hand" at work.

A great historical example of how both types of societies worked was East and West Germany after World War II – both with similar geographies and heritage – but with very different economies. West Germany, with a capitalistic bent, prospered, and recovered from the war well. Decades after the war had ended, East Germany, with its more socialist economy, was still struggling. Bombed out buildings from the war had not been replaced, and basic necessities were hard to come by. Many people sought a way out of the struggling country, often risking their lives to do it. This is the clear difference between a centrally planned society and a free market one.

Lesson Eighteen - "Middlemen" – Meddlesome or Useful?

Middlemen do the very important service of getting products from the producers to the consumers – the distribution portion of our market model. It would be very inefficient indeed for every consumer to have to meet with every producer to obtain their product.

Middlemen help facilitate the process as Bastiat explained it well: *"When the hungry stomach is at Paris, and corn which can satisfy it is at Odessa, the suffering cannot cease till the corn is brought into contact with the stomach. There are three means by which this contact may be affected. First the famished men go themselves and fetch the corn. Second they may leave this task to those whose trade it belongs to. Third they may club together and give the office in charge to public functionaries."*

Most of the time we are not interested in going to each farm to pick up our food, each factory to pick up our manufactured goods, etc. We would generally prefer to pay middlemen to transport those goods from the point of production closer to our point of consumption.

Bastiat continued, *"In every time, in all countries, and the more free, enlightened, and experienced they are, men have voluntarily chosen the second…The competition which they create amongst each other leads them no less irresistibly to cause the consumers to partake of the profits of those realized savings.*

The (corn) arrives; it is to the interest of commerce to sell it as soon as possible, so as to avoid risks, to realize its funds, and begin again the next opportunity. Directed by the comparison of prices, it distributes food over the whole surface of the country, beginning always at the highest price, that is where the demand is the greatest."

As Bastiat explained, when we can choose, we generally choose the middleman – not the government and generally not ourselves – to serve the critical role of distribution.

But what is our alternative to that well-working system, he asks? *"If according to the Socialist invention, the State were to stand in the stead of commerce, what would happen? I should like to be informed where the savings would be to the public? Would it be in the price of purchase? …Would the saving be in the expenses? …Would it be in the profits of the merchants? …And then consider the difficulty of levying so many taxes and of dividing so much food. Think of the injustice, of the abuses inseparable from such an enterprise. Think of the responsibility which would weigh upon the Government."*

Yet, today, there are so many who want to see our Government given more and more responsibilities in these regards, as if they could somehow do a better job than the market has done.

Lesson Nineteen – Speculators and Farmers – Friend or Foe?

Speculators are yet another important part of the economy that are often demonized in the media and in politics. Even conservatives don't always get it. A conservative talk show host once said, *"As you know, I've been very critical of the oil companies jacking up gas prices when there is plenty of supply available…I've criticized the President for doing nothing…when he could…get behind legislation to limit oil speculation."*

But speculators are another important aspect of the market. Speculators buy underpriced stocks that they expect to rise in price in the near future. If the stocks are truly undervalued, the actions of the speculators will help move them up in price, by increasing the demand. When speculators do sell, they increase the supply of those stocks again, and bring the prices back down. Speculation takes place in many areas, but two common ones are oil and food.

Speculators are not the enemies of those industries – they are friends – they bear the risks of the fluctuating farm (or oil) prices – and the rewards if and when the prices do rise. (Keeping the farmers from having to bear all these risks themselves.) When speculators sell, supply increases and prices drop.

As Fred Schnaubelt says in *Romancing the Voters*, *"To summarize. Speculators provide a valuable service when buying into anticipated shortages with the intention of profiting. They bring supply and demand into equilibrium, they induce people to consume less, supplies last longer, nearly always there is some supply without standing in line, plus, they create incentives for new supplies to climb sharply, after which prices drop."*

But when the government pays farmers to destroy crops or keep crops off the market with taxpayer money – those specific producers are helped, but at the harm of all consumers, since one result is that prices go up, so there is less money for consumers to spend elsewhere.

Hazlitt explained it very clearly: *"To give farmers money for restricting production, or to give them the same amount of money for an artificially restricted production; is no different from forcing consumers or taxpayers to pay people for doing nothing at all."*

In short we should reconsider our dislike of speculators and our infatuation with farm subsidies.

Lesson Twenty – The High Price of Interest Rates

Interest rates (especially high ones) also receive bad press often, as if they were somehow the result of someone being taken advantage of. But we have to first ask with Bastiat, *"What is interest?"* He answered for us: *"It is the service rendered, after a free[26] bargain, by the borrower to the lender, in remuneration for the service he has received by the loan."* In other words, interest is the price we pay to borrow money, or the price we are paid when we loan money. (Interest, as with other expenses, are a cost to one party and income to the other.)

Bastiat continued: *"By what law is the rate of these remunerative services established? By the general law which regulates the equivalent of all services; that is, by the law of supply and demand."* Here we see supply and demand coming into play yet again. Bastiat reminded us that in loans there is an *"actual service rendered by the lender, and which makes the borrower liable to an equivalent service, two services, whose comparative value can only be appreciated, like that of all possible services, by freedom."* In other words, the borrower profits by a loan as much as the lender does, or he would not take the loan.

Again, Bastiat explained, *"Interest is not injurious to the borrower...the transaction cannot be accomplished without the consent of the one as well as of the other."* If interest rates are too high in a free market, the borrower has the right not to take the loan, and eventually someone else will come along and offer lower interest rates, because *"The more easily a thing is procured the smaller is the service rendered by yielding it or lending it...It is not surprising, therefore, that the more abundant capitals are, the lower is the interest."*

As we can see from Bastiat's quotes it was already clear more than one hundred and fifty years ago that markets best regulated interest rates.

---

[26] Free as in "free choice," not as in "no cost."

They should be tied to supply and demand – the quantity of money available to be lent, the demand for it, and the risks involved in loaning it. As with anything else, if the price (interest rates in this case) is kept too low, the demand will outpace the supply and there will be a shortage. The market can effectively regulate that – but the government cannot. When the government interferes in the form of overly low interest rates, it will lead to unsustainable growth, or booms. These artificial booms will be followed by busts – we see it time and again!

Remember, money that is lent by banks was first saved or invested by someone. Saving starts when an individual chooses to save rather than consume all of their income. With investments, someone has chosen to invest a portion of their excess income to generate future income.

Saving does not equal hoarding. When money is saved it allows others to put that money to use – often to increase production.

One last thought on saving: You may read somewhere that saving causes depressions. But saving in those cases is not the cause of depressions – it is the result of depression. In those situations people are refusing to buy in the short term because they fear that prices will continue to go down signfiicantly in the near future.

Lesson Twenty-One – Property Rights

Samuel Adams, patriot and founding father, once said: *"Among the natural rights of the colonists are these: First a right to life, secondly to liberty, and thirdly to property: together with the right to defend them in the best manner they can."*[27]

Samuel Adams

The following century Bastiat noted, *"Property does not exist because there are laws, but laws exist because there is property."*

And more recently President Calvin Coolidge explained it as, *"Ultimately property rights and personal rights are the same thing."*

President Coolidge

Contrast these with what Karl Marx once said: *"The theory of the Communists may be summed up in the single sentence: Abolition of private property."*

Proponents of the free market understand that the rights to our property – to consume it or to distribute it as we see fit – are an important function in a free society. The freer a society, the more secure a man's right to his own property will be. In fact, one of the most important concepts in economically-sound societies is the idea of property rights. If we don't own it, can we ever really build on it, improve it, or create with it? Where is our incentive if we don't have the rights to our own property?

As we spoke of earlier, the Pilgrims tried a very brief and quite unsuccessful attempt at limiting property rights. Famine and hunger increased, rather than decreasing, in this perfect example of "the tragedy of the commons." The solution was simple and effective: families were given their own plots of land and the responsibilities and rights that went with them.

---

[27] There is a wonderful www.Izzit.org DVD, *Who Owns What?* that deals with property rights. It has sections on "The Tragedy of Urban Renewal," "D.C. Taxi Heist," "Battle for the California Desert," and "How to Save a Dying Ocean."

The alternative to the government protecting our property rights is the government being complicit in the act of plunder. It is hard to put it better than Bastiat said it over 150 years ago: *"...Man recoils from trouble--from suffering; and yet he is condemned by nature to the suffering of privation, if he does not take the trouble to work. He has to choose, then, between these two evils. What means can he adopt to avoid both? There remains now, and there will remain, only one way, which is, to enjoy the labor of others..."*

"This is the origin of slavery and of plunder, whatever its form may be--whether that of wars, impositions, violence, restrictions, frauds, etc.--monstrous abuses, but consistent with the thought which has given them birth. Oppression should be detested and resisted--it can hardly be called absurd."

"Before I proceed, I think I ought to explain myself upon the word plunder. I do not take it, as it often is taken, in a vague, undefined, relative, or metaphorical sense. I use it in its scientific acceptation, and as expressing the opposite idea to property. When a portion of wealth passes out of the hands of him who has acquired it, without his consent, and without compensation, to him who has not created it, whether by force or by artifice, I say that property is violated, that plunder is perpetrated." And I could not agree with him more.

Continuing, Bastiat said, *"When law and force keep a man within the bounds of justice, they impose nothing upon him but a mere negation. They only oblige him to abstain from doing harm. They violate neither his personality his liberty, nor his property. They only guard the personality, the liberty, the property of others. They hold themselves on the defensive; they defend the equal right of all...A friend of mine once remarked to me, to say that the aim of the law is to cause justice to reign, is to use an expression which is not rigorously exact. It ought to be said, the aim of the law is to prevent injustice from reigning...It is not justice which has an existence of its own, it is injustice. The one results from the absence of the other."*

So, government should exist to protect us from injustice, but is that the way most people see it today?[28]

---

[28] For more on Bastiat's wisdom on Legalized Plunder, see *Appendix #4 – Wealth Redistribution*.

Lesson Twenty-Two – Rule of Law

Most of us take laws, and the need for laws, for granted. But Bastiat explained their role in a new way: *"It is not because men have made laws, that personality, liberty, and property exist. On the contrary, it is because personality, liberty, and property exist beforehand, that men make laws. Nature, or rather God, has bestowed upon every one of us the right to defend his person, his liberty, and his property, since these are the three constituent or preserving elements of life; elements, each of which is rendered complete by the others, and cannot be understood without them."*

The idea that our rights come first and then laws to protect them will follow strikes some as unusual. But I think Bastiat has it right. He continues, *"…Now, labor being in itself a pain, and man being naturally inclined to avoid pain, it follows, and history proves it, that wherever plunder is less burdensome than labor, it prevails; and neither religion nor morality can, in this case, prevent it from prevailing. When does plunder cease, then? When it becomes less burdensome and more dangerous than labour."*

This gets back to what we said earlier about incentives. Law, and government, should incentivize individuals to work – not to plunder. *"It is very evident that the proper aim of law is to oppose the powerful obstacle of collective force to this fatal tendency; that all its measures should be in favor of property, and against plunder.…It would be impossible, therefore, to introduce into society a greater change and a greater evil than this--the conversion of the law into an instrument of plunder."*

Bastiat agrees with what we have been saying earlier – government exists to protect property; governments should exist to protect us from plunder, not to legalize plunder!

"…No society can exist unless the laws are respected to a certain degree, but the safest way to make them respected is to make them respectable. When law and morality are in contradiction to each other, the citizen finds himself in the cruel alternative of either losing his moral sense, or of losing his respect for the law--two evils of equal magnitude, between which it would be difficult to choose."

Without respectable laws a country is encouraging (incentivizing) its citizens not to be law-abiding citizens!

"...Look at the United States. There is no country in the world where the law is kept more within its proper domain--which is, to secure to everyone his liberty and his property."

If this could be said of us in 1850, can it still be said of us in 2013? *"Therefore, there is no country in the world where social order appears to rest upon a more solid basis.*

"Nevertheless, even in the United States, there are two questions, and only two, which from the beginning have endangered political order. And what are these two questions? That of slavery and that of tariffs; that is, precisely the only two questions in which, contrary to the general spirit of this republic, law has taken the character of a plunderer. Slavery is a violation, sanctioned by law, of the rights of the person..."

Prior to the Civil War, Bastiat saw our biggest problems in the U.S. as slavery and tariffs. Slavery is no longer legal, but what has replaced it? With taxes ever on the rise, aren't we becoming slaves to the government now instead?

Lesson Twenty-Three – What's Fair?

One of the episodes of Milton Friedman's "Free to Choose" series[29] was called "Created Equal." There he spoke of Jefferson's words in the Declaration of Independence: *"We hold these truths to be self-evident that all men are created equal. They are endowed by their creator…"*

Friedman pointed out that it is a myth that the rich have benefited at the expense of the poor. As he stated so well, *"Nothing could be further from the truth. Wherever the free market has been permitted to operate, the ordinary man has been able to attain levels of living never dreamed of before."*

And that's exactly what we saw in Rosling's video, "200 countries, 200 years, 4 minutes."

Friedman went on to explain an interesting paradox: *"The inheritance of talent is no different from an ethical point of view from the inheritance of other forms of property, of bonds, of stocks, of houses or of factories. Yet many people resent the one but not the other."*

Then he went on to explain a dangerous shift in thinking from the 19th to the 20th century. After the Civil War there was a push for *"equality of opportunities"* consistent with the concept of freedom. But in the 20th century the ideal shifted to *"the idea that the economic race should be so arranged that everybody ends at the finish line at the same time rather than that everyone starts at the beginning at the same time."*

But if we are trying to "level the playing field" in this way, it brings everybody down – it doesn't bring anyone up! In spite of that, many government decisions in our country seem to be based on "class envy" or a supposed need for people "paying their fair share."

But does class envy make sense in a country like ours? We are not some sort of a caste society where people are stuck in one place or another. In the U.S. the terms "lower income" and "middle income" are much more meaningful than "lower class" or "middle class."

As opposed to in some societies, here people do move from one income level to another, and many

---

[29] www.Izzit.org has a DVD about Friedman's economic ideas, "Free or Equal." There is also quite a bit more on his economic philosophy on www.FreeToChoose.Tv.

will do exactly that over the course of their lifetimes. When we make less money than someone else, that should not cause envy, but rather rejoicing that we have the opportunity to attain that level as well. Does that seem unbelievable to you? See what the Federal Reserve has discovered:

The Federal Reserve divides income levels into quintiles (i.e. five equally proportioned groups). Their studies of income mobility show that even those in the lowest quintile (lowest 20%) of income or those in the highest 20% do not always remain there. According to a recent study they did, 58% of those in the lowest quintile of income moved to a higher quintile in a ten year period, and 50% of the wealthiest dropped to a lower quintile.

In our country even the poorest live better than much of the rest of the world. Of the 15% of the U.S. population that our government considers living in poverty, 80% have air conditioning, and almost 75% own at least one car. Most homes in the United States, regardless of income, have multiple televisions, a microwave, a refrigerator, oven, and washing machine. Yes, there are certainly poor who suffer, but "living in poverty" in the United States does not generally equate to suffering.

Early in the 20th century Mises wrote of an even more startling difference over time: *"Today, in the capitalist countries there is relatively little difference between the basic life of the so-called higher and lower classes; both have food, clothing, and shelter. But in the 18th century and earlier, the difference...was that the man of the middle class had shoes and the man of the lower class did not have shoes."*

In spite of all this, there are many who would like to see the government redistribute wealth to "help" alleviate that poverty, as if having "the rich" pay their fair share will somehow even all these things out.

"Rich" people already pay more taxes (and a higher percentage) than poor people. For those crying for them to pay their "fair share," I ask: at what point will they be considered to be paying their fair share: 60%, 70%, 80%? Even if we continued to raise the rates on the rich there are not enough of "them" to fund all the government programs that people can imagine.

What we're really accomplishing here is simply a "redistribution of wealth," and we should call it what it is. And going back to Rosling's video, and our earlier lesson we see that moving the standard of living up for an entire society is what helps the poor — not redistributing the wealth of "the rich."

As British Prime Minister Margaret Thatcher once said, *"The problem with socialism is that you eventually run out of other people's money."*

Prime Minister Thatcher

Even President John F. Kennedy (a Democratic president in the 1960's) understood the problem with higher and higher tax rates: *"An economy hampered by restrictive tax rates will never produce enough revenue to balance our budget, just as it will never produce enough jobs or enough profits."*

President Kennedy

About forty years before that President Calvin Coolidge explained, *"The wise and correct course to follow in taxation and all other economic legislation is not to destroy those who have already secured success but to create conditions under which everyone will have a better chance to be successful."*

But in spite of the wisdom handed down through the ages of those who have understood these basic concepts there have always been some who want the government to practice "plunder" as Bastiat described it:

"What can be better calculated to silence our scruples, and, which is perhaps better appreciated, to overcome all resistance? We all, therefore, put in our claim, under some pretext or other, and apply to Government. We say to it, 'I am dissatisfied at the proportion between my labor and my enjoyments. I should like, for the sake of restoring the desired equilibrium, to take a part of the possessions of others. But this would be dangerous. Could not you facilitate the thing for me?

"Could you not find me a good place? or check the industry of my competitors? or, perhaps, lend me gratuitously some capital, which you may take from its possessor? Could you not bring up my children at the public expense? or grant me some prizes? or secure me a competence when I have attained my fiftieth year? By this means I shall gain my end with an easy conscience, for the law will have acted for me, and I shall have all the advantages of plunder, without its risk or its disgrace!'"

But is plunder by the government really so different than that by outlaws, except that it is harder to fight against?

Years later Mises explained it well, *"What those people who ask for equality have in mind is always an increase in their own power to consume. In endorsing the principle of equality as a political postulate nobody wants to share his own income with those who have less...When the American wage earner refers to equality, he means that the dividends of the stockholders should be given to him. He does not suggest a curtailment of his own income for the benefit of 95 percent of the earth's population whose income is lower than his."*

We should remember these ideas when people are complaining that the rich need to "pay their fair share."

Lesson Twenty-Four – Public vs. Private Services

We are often taught that public services are somehow better than private ones, and yet if we remember that public services actually only come by force, we may be in a better position to evaluate the difference.

Going back to the importance of "seen and unseen" Bastiat explained, *"Society is the total of the forced or voluntary services which men perform for each other; that is to say, of public services and private services...You will understand that a public enterprise is a coin with two sides. Upon one is engraved a laborer at work, with this device, that which is seen; on the other is a laborer out of work, with the device, that which is not seen."*

As we said before, when the government is doing something, it actually gets in the way of private citizens doing it. Whether we are talking about assistance after a storm or caring for the elderly – these are all things private citizen used to expect to do.

Additionally there is a large divide between those who are in favor of a constrained government and those who prefer an unconstrained form of government in regards to governmental responsibilities. We could ask, what should our taxes be paying for? What should government provide? The debates rages now, but it is not a new debate, as these Bastiat's words from over 150 years ago show us: *"...Socialism, like the old policy from which it emanates, confounds Government and society. And so, every time we object to a thing being done by Government, it concludes that we object to its being done at all. We disapprove of education by the State--then we are against education altogether. We object to a State religion--then we would have no religion at all. We object to an equality which is brought about by the State--then we are against equality, etc., etc. They might as well accuse us of wishing men not to eat, because we object to the cultivation of corn by the State."*

When I first read this we had just been involved in this argument in one of my classes. Someone had proposed abolishing the Department of Education. Those who were aghast at the idea accused those who favored it of being against education!

But that was not their position – they were merely against education being provided by the state (along with food, housing, medical care, and today the list goes on).

Bastiat continued, *"How is it that the strange idea of making the law produce what it does not contain--prosperity, in a positive sense, wealth, science, religion--should ever have gained ground in the political world?"* There seems to be an even greater push now for government to grant these things to its citizens.

But in order for the government to provide more and more "benefits" it must continue to consume more and more of its citizens' income in taxes.

Additionally, government spending takes money away from where those in the private sector would have put it, and put it in places the private sector would not have. For instance, if the private sector does not yet value solar panels, how does it make sense for the government to put taxpayer money there?

So maybe we should rethink the difference between public and private projects and realize that public projects are still being paid for by taxpayer money.

Lesson Twenty-Five – Cost, Size and Role of Government

Building on the last lesson, remember Bastiat's words, *"Government is the great fiction through which everybody endeavors to live at the expense of everybody else."* Something "free" from the government never really is; anything given away as "entitlements" has to first be taken from someone else.

Benjamin Franklin

Benjamin Franklin once wrote: *"I am for doing good to the poor, but...I think the best way of doing good to the poor, is not making them easy in poverty, but leading or driving them out of it. I observed...that the more public provisions were made for the poor, the less they provided for themselves, and of course became poorer. And, on the contrary, the less was done for them, the more they did for themselves, and became richer."*

If an individual took our money against our will, we would call it stealing, but when the government takes it by force, they call it taxes. But what's the real difference? Yes, some taxes are necessary to run the government, but as we said before: when it actually amounts to the redistribution of wealth, there is nothing in the Constitution to support that.

In addition to constitutional issues, one of the first things we should ask when anyone talks about the government doing something (at the local, state, or federal level): "How much will it cost and who is going to pay for it?"

President Ford

As we determine how big we think government should be, we should take to heart President Gerald Ford's words: *"A government big enough to give you everything you want is a government big enough to take from you everything you have."*

This is not a 20th or 21st century philosophy. We even had congressmen who believed this going back to our country's early days. Senator Henry Clay once said, *"Government is a trust, and the officers of the government are trustees. And both the trust and the trustees are created for the benefit of the people."*[30]

Senator Clay

That would be for the benefit of all people, not merely a select group.

Sometimes we seem to forget that the Declaration of Independence talks about the right to *"life, liberty,* **and the pursuit of happiness"** – not *"life, liberty,* **and happiness."**

Government's role should never be to make us happy.

President Thomas Jefferson, our third president, understood the distinction, even if some of our recent ones haven't: *"I predict future happiness for Americans, if they can prevent the government from wasting the labors of the people under the pretense of taking care of them."* He also stated, *"My reading of history convinces me that most bad government results from too much government."*

Bastiat pulled no punches when he described government and what it can and cannot accomplish: *"I should be glad enough, you may be sure, if you had really discovered a beneficent and inexhaustible being, calling itself the Government, which has bread for all mouths, work for all hands, capital for all enterprises, credit for all projects, oil for all wounds…a universal physician, an unlimited treasure, and an infallible counselor, such as you describe Government to be…For no one would think of asserting that this precious discovery has yet been made."*

They hadn't discovered such a thing by the mid-19th century, and they haven't discovered it yet!

For more of Bastiat's wisdom on the role of government, please see **Appendix #5** – *Government: Universal Physician? Unlimited Treasure? Infallible Counselor?* And please don't forget that resources and wealth are not created by government, they are merely redistributed.

---

[30] Henry Clay, U.S. Representative & Senator from Kentucky in the 18th century.

Lesson Twenty-Six – Disastrous Debt and Deficits

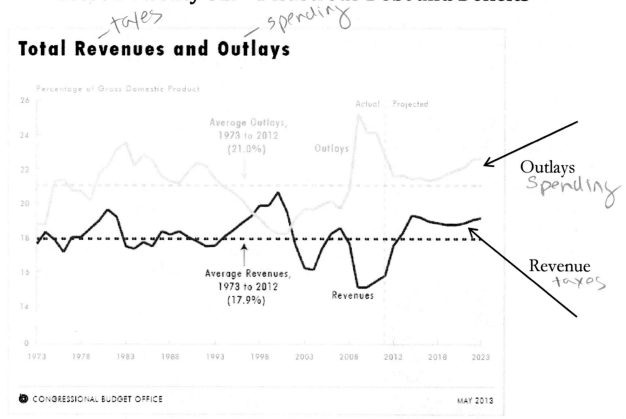

Budget deficit is spending more than is taken in.

Debt is the total amount owed (which increases with the interest added).

Surplus is when revenues are higher than spending – something that has happened in the past, but not in a long time!

As you can see from the above chart, in the last thirty years there have usually been extremely large gaps between the outlays (spending) by the Federal Government and the revenue that it has collected. Each year where the outlays have exceeded the revenue represent a budget deficit. And each deficit has increased the amount of debt owed by the United States.

As we said previously, the government has no money of its own. It must raise money through taxes, budget deficits, or inflation.

When the federal government borrows money to pay for programs it cannot currently afford, it is stealing from future generations. A balanced budget would be one of the greatest gifts we could give to our children and grandchildren.

This, too, is not a new concept. President Jefferson, the third president of the United States remarked, *"I, however, place economy among the first and most important republican virtues, and public debt as the greatest of the dangers to be feared."*

President Jefferson

Yet today it seems that people have become comfortable with our national debt. But a country should no more spend money it doesn't have than a family should. Smith put it this way, *"What is prudence in the conduct of every private family can scarce be folly in that of a great kingdom."*

As we have seen the country's deficit, and therefore our debt, continue to rise at alarming rates, we should wonder how future generations will feel about paying for today's programs.

For more on how the Federal Government currently budgets and spends your tax dollars, see ***Appendix #6*** – *Money, Power, and Control through Federal Budgets and Executive Departments.*

Lesson Twenty-Seven – Risks and Uncertainties

Much is made of the (high) profits a company might make, but it is unusual to hear the same concern for a company's losses. A business by its very nature entails risk; risk commonly felt by the entrepreneur and/or the stock holders. There is the hope in a new company (or even an existing one) that income will surpass expenses. But the risk that it will not always exists.

Risks are not a bad thing; they are a very important part of life.[31] The dilemma becomes when government tries to override risks. They can't get rid of the uncertainties – unless they forbid business from taking risks, but they can transfer those risks to society as a whole. That's what happened before the housing boom and bust when the government was meddling with mortgages; it's what has happened more recently with a number of solar companies.

But in a free market, we allow a business to assume its own risks – and the losses that might occur (or the profits that might occur). This is as it should be. Entrepreneurs are risking their own money, or the money of someone who has entrusted it to them – that they are directly responsible to.

Therefore they are generally more responsive to the market and watch for ways to minimize losses and maximize profits. The same cannot be said of the government. When the government misspends taxpayer money, we are seldom able to hold it accountable. Instead it just takes more money and continues the cycle.

When the risks are particularly high in a specific industry there are often proposals that the government should assume these risks. But Hazlitt explained the difficulty with that type of thinking:

"This means that bureaucrats should be permitted to take risk with the taxpayers' money that no one is willing to take with his own. Such a policy would lead to evils of many different kinds. It would lead to favoritism: to the making of loans to friends, or in return for bribes...It would increase the

---

[31]For an excellent book on risk, see Dr. Ben Carson's book, *Take the Risk: Learning to Identify, Choose, and Live with Acceptable Risk.*

demand for socialism…In the case of government-lending the money is that of other people, and it has been taken from them, regardless of their personal wish, in taxes. The private money will be invested only where repayment with interest or profit is definitely expected….Private loans will utilize existing resources and capital far better than government loans."

Individuals and businesses should be allowed to make their own decisions and assume their own risks. As President Reagan once said, "Government exists to protect us from each other. Where government has gone beyond its limits is in deciding to protect us from ourselves."

President Reagan

Lesson Twenty-Eight – Competition vs. Monopolies

A short but important lesson:

Competition equals "active demand for two or more goods in short supply." Competition protects customers **and** workers!

Competition is a very important part of the free market process. It is the key to the price-supply-demand triad. When prices go down and demand goes up, it's competition that encourages other producers to get into that market. It is competition that keeps shortages from occurring, or at least from staying a reality for very long. Competition keeps a producer from raising prices too high. In other words, it prevents true price gouging.

Price gouging is the idea of retailers raising their prices unfairly. Cries of price gouging are often heard after a natural disaster – when retailers are trying to raise their prices to meet the quickly rising demand. If competition exists, those prices will not go too high or stay too high.

Smith explained that competition results in *"allocating productive resources to their most-valued uses."* This gets back to the profit-motive. Profits will help keep resources where will do the most good.

In short, competition is a beautiful thing. You might ask then why we have shortages or other difficulties that competition should solve. In short, it is government intervention that short circuits competition. When the government allows a business (or itself) to have a monopoly in an area, it smothers competition. With a monopoly we will quickly find rising prices and/or limited supply.

For instance, when the government has the monopoly on electrical or water supplies – they prevent others from coming in and offering the same product at a better price or a better product at the same price.

Supposedly in order to prevent monopolies, anti-trust laws have been passed in the United States that outlaw monopolies and monopolistic behavior – artificially raising prices and limiting output.

But anti-trust laws have actually been used to harass legitimate companies (like Standard Oil in 1911). We should follow the lead of other countries – and a true free market – and let competition regulate prices and supplies, not the government!

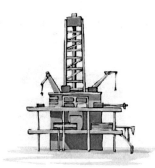

Lesson Twenty-Nine – Government Intervention through Price-Fixing

We spoke briefly in an earlier lesson about prices and their effect on supply and demand in a free market. As we said then, price should signal changes in supply and demand. So when do we have a problem? It's when something interferes with the balance of the triad – generally price distortions in the form of price controls.

When the government sets a price floor prices are forced higher than they would have been without government intervention. The higher prices lead to supplies rising further than the demand, causing a glut.

A prime example of this is minimum wages. There the government has artificially set the price of certain labor too high causing supplies of labor to exceed the demand for it. The predictable result is a surplus of labor, which equals unemployment.

When the government does the opposite and sets a price ceiling, there is an artificial limit to how high prices can be raised. So what happens when demand goes up quickly or significantly for that item? An example of price ceilings is the ceilings California placed on electricity prices. The artificially lower prices resulted in too much demand; the predictable result was blackouts.

Another prime example of this is rent control. With rent control the government limits the amount of rent that can be charged for certain properties in certain areas. Again, with the artificially low prices, demand goes up, but the supply won't rise to meet the demand. So instead of helping those who needed cheaper housing options, a shortage will occur, making it even more difficult for them to find adequate housing at a reasonable price.

In an attempt to fix the new issues, the government may try rationing, cost control, subsidies, and/or universal price fixing. None of these are effective measures.

Through rationing the government may try to do what a free market would have done through the prices. It may limit the demand that way, but it can't stimulate the supply, as Hazlitt expressed so well: *"When prices are arbitrarily held down by government compulsion, demand is chronically in excess of supply."*

The government may try to hold down the prices of some of the things that go into producing the first commodity, it further spreads the problem, it doesn't solve it).

Or they may pay subsidies to the producers. But this is merely subsidizing the producers by the consumers. Hazlitt had this to say about subsidies: *"Subsidies are paid for by someone, and no method has been discovered by which the community gets something for nothing."* Sowell also explained, *"Subsidies have further repercussions that can make the country as a whole worse off."*

Farm subsidies are a common form of government subsidy. But it must be remembered that any money government spends on subsidies come from someone else. There can be no "winners" in this situation without an equivalent amount of "losers."

Ultimately, if prices are rising there is either a surplus of money or a scarcity of goods, neither of which will be solved by price-fixing.

As conservatives, we believe that government should be about security – the preservation of order – not interfering with the market! In fact, Mises explained, *"Interventionism means that the government not only fails to protect the smooth functions of the market economy, but that it interferes with prices, with wage rates, interest rates, and profits."*

Mises continued, *"The idea of government interference as a solution to economic problems leads in every country, to conditions which at the least, are very unsatisfactory and often quite chaotic. If the government does not stop in time, it will bring on socialism."*

And this is clearly the direction the United States is heading if we continue with increased amounts of government intervention in the market.

Lesson Thirty – Minimum Wages

It must be remembered that wages are a price. As such, they will be paid by someone. Minimum Wages is one of the best known and least understood of the price **floors** set by the government.

Lower wages are often degraded because they are "not enough to live off." But people making minimum wage (or lower, if it were legal) are not bound to stay at that pay rate forever. Their starting rate is exactly that, a starting rate that can help an unskilled or low skilled worker get started along the path of employment. As opposed to in a caste-type society, our current wages are not a life sentence (or a death sentence). Low wages are often meant to be "learning wages."[32] A low paying job is often merely the first step of many on a wage ladder that goes up and up.

But as a result of politicians' continuing push to raise minimum wage higher and higher, large groups of people have become routinely unemployed, particularly minorities and teens.

Hazlitt explained the problem well: *"You cannot make a man worth a given amount by making it illegal for anyone to offer him anything less. You merely deprive him of the right to earn the amount that his abilities and situation would permit him to earn, while you deprive the community even of the moderate services that he is capable of rendering. In brief, for a low wage you substitute unemployment."*

Contrast Hazlitt's thoughts with the politician who recently said, *"If we started in 1960...then the minimum wage today would be about $22 an hour"* [33] But what would a minimum wage of $22 per hour accomplish? (Or a $35 per hour minimum as the New York labor unions want?) Just more unemployment, as Hazlitt explained.

As we discussed earlier, earning minimum wage is not a permanent state. Minimum wage earners who read and write English seldom stay at minimum wage for more than a year. But, sadly, they do become a useful political tool for those who want to cry foul about the lack of "living wages" provided for by wages that are "too low."[34]

---

[32] As Fred Schnaubelt put it so well in his book, *Romancing the Voters*.
[33] Senator Elizabeth Warren

[34] For a great article on the damage of raising minimum wage, see the article on www.FEE.org on minimum wages.

Lesson Thirty-One – Price Gouging

As we discussed, whenever there is a major storm, the likes of Hurricane Katrina, the tornadoes that devastated much of the southeast in 2011, and more recently, SuperStorm Sandy, there is always talk of price gouging. We hear it at all levels – from the President, from state governors and city mayors, to name the most visible.

But let's examine what happens with a storm and what "price gouging" really is. The undeniable facts are that after a major catastrophe like any of these storms, there is an increase in demand for certain items (usually starting with generators, gas, food, and water, but depending on the event, the list could go on to include plywood, sandbags, flashlights, etc.).

But the specific items are not the real issue. The real issue is that after a storm (or even just before) the demand for these things rise. With a rise in demand, only two things can occur right away – a rise in price or shortages. Is there a third option? Nope, not in the short term! In the longer term supplies can be increased to match the increase in demand, but that will not (because it cannot) happen in the short term. A rise in demand always triggers a rise in prices or shortages.

So let's go back to our recent storm and this talk of price gouging. The governor (or other misinformed leader) declares that raising prices in the midst of (or recovery from) a storm is profiteering improperly from the storm and such profiteers will be soundly punished. Businesses are told, "No, you may not raise your prices on those items at all." So, with no increase in prices, what has to happen? Yes, shortages. They happen every time. Not just some of the time, every time. They are as predictable as the cries of price gouging.

So, instead of being able to pay more for the gas you need for your car or your generator, you won't be able to get any at all. Instead of paying more for the food or water you need, the stores will simply run out.

But think for a bit what the alternative would be like if we encouraged gas stations and grocery stores to raise their prices as needed after a storm, and applauded them for that instead of vilifying them. What would the situation be like then? If you were the 100th person in the store, or the 1000th person, you might actually be able to buy a few cans of tuna or some bottled water; there might be batteries still on the shelf, and gasoline at the pump. Yes, you would have to pay more for them, but you would be able to purchase what you absolutely needed. If it's a true need you would be thrilled to be paying double rather than not being able to purchase those items at all!

In time, supplies can go up to take care of these increased demands. But let's consider how quickly supplies will go up if prices are kept artificially low, versus if they are allowed to rise to the new market level.

Given the opportunity, the people in the next town or county or state are more likely to bring more of (fill in the blank with whatever it is you need and can't buy after the storm) and sell it at a higher price in your area than they can sell it back home. But if the government has put a price ceiling on what those items can be sold for, there is no (I repeat, no) incentive for someone to work harder (and pay more) to bring items to a hard-hit area rather than just to stay where they are and sell them for the same price.

Yes, they may do it out of the goodness of their heart, but then we're talking about charity, not business.

So, rather than sitting back and hoping that the government will bring in the needed supplies, or some relief agency will show up with something that is desperately needed, we should also unleash the power of the market to assist!

Let those prices go up, don't demonize those who may profit by filling a need, and watch how quickly the demand and the supply will equalize again after the storm!

The alternative to price gouging or shortages is more government intervention. But what is government intervention after a storm or other tragedy other than again transferring wealth from one section of society to another? True, there are people in need – but at what point did we accept/expect the government to be their solution?

There is a great story of Davy Crockett when he was a congressman in the early 19th century. The story is about him giving a speech to Congress when he was voting against a bill for the government to provide charity to widows. Whether he actually gave the "Not Yours to Give" speech or not, the story is quite instructive about what the role of government should and shouldn't be at such times.[35] His bottom line was that individuals should help other individuals out, the government should not.

Davy Crockett

In the late 19th century President Grover Cleveland vetoed a small sum of money that was to go to assist a community after a disaster. He wrote of his veto, *"While it is the duty of the citizens to support the government, it is not the duty of the government to support the citizens."*

President Cleveland

Along those lines, if the government does "good" with our money, it prevents **us** from doing good with that same money.

Since the days of Davy Crockett and President Cleveland attitudes have clearly shifted significantly. But again, it could be asked, where is the constitutional ability of the government to do these things, even "good" things?

---

[35] You can find the story and the speech at www.FEE.org.

Lesson Thirty-Two – Rationing & Black Markets

Another short, but important, lesson:

A **Black Market** is a market where the goods that are bought and sold are either illegal, or where the goods are being sold illegally (around trade restrictions, etc.)

Rationing occurs when the government artificially restricts any particular raw materials, goods, or services.

As stated before, when supplies don't keep up with demand, we end up with shortages. Those shortages can be short term if the free market is given a chance to work. But if the government intervenes, as it so often does, those shortages are often longer term. One way governments deal with long-term shortages is through rationing (legally limiting the quantity that an individual can purchase of a good or goods).

Often when the government interferes with supply and demand too much through price-fixing or rationing, black markets develop to fill the needs. In fact, during and after World War II many Europeans were kept alive by black markets.

But black markets cause a number of issues, including the fact that businesses and consumers then become accustomed to breaking the law – a legal and a moral dilemma.

Many people act as if rationing is somehow more virtuous than raising prices (which will cause people to ration on their own according to their true needs and wants). Government rationing, on the other hand, sets arbitrary limits, which may not take into consideration real needs.

In the black market, goods are finding their way to those who demand them, around the government-approved channels. All of this should lead us to ask: Who would we rather have solve shortage issues, the free market, the government, or the black market?

Lesson Thirty-Three – Unemployment and Unions

Once upon a time unions accomplished an important service for their workers – improving working conditions and bringing working hours down to what may reasonably be considered a healthier limit.

But since then the primary "accomplishment" of unions has been to raise the wages of their workers above the market level. As we saw with minimum wages, there is a direct result of these wage increases – a corresponding increase in unemployment. They also raise production costs and generally force the least efficient business out of business.

At the same time, much is made of the need to lower unemployment rates. But, one of the primary barriers to higher employment rates is minimum wage rates and arbitrarily high union wages. While it is a laudable goal to provide a job for everyone who would like one, Hazlitt points out that a country's goal should be full production, from which full employment will come.

When unions strike for higher wages they are interfering with the free market to the extent that they don't allow current employees to continue working or new employees ("strikebreakers" or "scabs") to accept the old wages. If the unions were correct that their members were truly being underpaid, there would be not one willing to take the jobs at the lower wages; but that is seldom the case.

If union workers do succeed in raising their wages, it is seldom the profits of the company that are affected, it is the prices everyone will pay for whatever goods that company produces.

Hazlitt wrote much about the damage done by unions. Unions have *"opposed payment on the basis of output or efficiency and insisted on the same hourly rates for all their members regardless of differences in productivity. They have insisted on promotion for seniority rather than for merit. They have initiated deliberate slowdowns, under the pretense of fighting speedups…*

They have opposed the introduction or improvement of machinery. They have insisted on make-work rules to require more people or more time to perform a given task. They have even insisted, with the threat of ruining employers, on the hiring of people who are not needed at all…their net effect has been to reduce productivity below what it would otherwise have been."

It appears safe to say that unions served a valuable purpose when they first came along and protected workers from long hours and dangerous workplaces. But they have gone far beyond that place today.

Lesson Thirty-Four – International Trade and Outsourcing

Imports (what we bring in from other countries) and exports (what we sell to other countries) are an important part of our national economy. (In reality imports and exports are actually individuals in our country buying from individuals in another country, but we generally discuss them as if they are one country trading with another.) Sadly, too many people act like exports are good for the country's economy and imports are somehow bad.

Hazlitt explained, *"Exceed only by the pathological dread of imports that affects all nations is a pathological yearning for exports. Logically…nothing could be more inconsistent. In the long run imports and exports must equal each other…It is exports that pay for imports and vice versa…When we decide to cut down our imports, we are in affect deciding also to cut down our exports."*

In fact, a big deal is often made of the "Balance of Trade" – the difference between what we export and what we import. Since all trade should be a win-win for both sides involved, balance of trade "deficits" cannot be a bad thing!

When tariffs (taxes on certain imported items) are put into effect they are there to protect domestic producers (of that particular item) at the expense of the consumers, who will now be forced to pay higher prices than they could have without tariffs. Tariffs also hurt other domestic producers who will suffer in their ability to export their products. (Import quotas cause the same problems by artificially limiting supplies, and thus also raising prices!)

As a result of tariffs Americans as a whole are worse off and our trading partners are worse off. So who benefits from tariffs? Only the producers – an example of special interests – who are now able to sell their products at a higher price than they could have (and arguably than they should have) without the tariffs.

Let's look at an example of how this works: In 2002 the U.S. Steel industry succeeded in getting tariffs imposed on imported steel. As a result of the tariffs the steel industry could raise their prices and increase their employment – but higher steel prices meant increased steel costs for industries that used steel – therefore reducing their profits and increasing their unemployment. Additionally, the countries that had been exporting steel to the U.S. retaliated by imposing their own tariffs on the United States.

The end result was actually an overall increase in prices paid by consumers; hardly the picture that was painted by those promoting tariffs.

Outsourcing

While it sounds good to say that as a country we should be independent, will that ever be the case? Should it be? Or should we strive for interdependence?

Another time our economy is interlinked with that of other countries is in outsourcing – the act of sending jobs overseas.

How many people oppose outsourcing because it sends "American" jobs overseas, but approve the idea of foreign aid? Outsourcing is the best form of foreign aid – helping a country through the power of the market.

Another complaint of outsourcing is that big corporations are taking advantage of employees in Third World countries by paying them less than they would have paid Americans for the same job. But this complaint fails to take into consideration an important point: When corporations offer jobs in Third World countries they are usually offering them at higher wages than people there could make at other jobs.

It could be asked why should we make things domestically (or do them domestically) if it's cheaper to import them.

Immigration

Another hot topic involving the United States and other countries is immigration – both legal and illegal. We won't go into it at length here, but when you hear discussions about immigration and immigration quotas, consider them in light of the economic principles you've been learning here – particularly supply and demand, and fair trade.

Lesson Thirty-Five – Recessions, Depressions, Inflation and Stagflation

Recession – When prices decline significantly for more than a few months (often labeled as such when GDP[36] goes down two quarters in a row).

Depression – A sustained, long term downturn (i.e. a severe recession that lasts more than two years).

Inflation – A sustained increase in the general price level in an economy (which leads to an increase in the cost of living).

Stagflation – Inflation accompanied by slow growth and high unemployment.

More on Inflation

There are some who somehow think that the supply of money can be increased without prices going up – but it doesn't happen! Indeed, there are two types of inflationists according to Hazlitt: Naïve ones who think twice as much money means we can buy twice as much. The second kind who think government can "solve all our problems merely by printing money…They would have it print just enough to make up some alleged 'deficiency' or 'gap.'"

Like other government interferences, one group will profit (at least in the short term) at the expense of all others. Hazlitt explained:

The most obvious and yet the oldest and most stubborn error on which the appeal of inflations rests is that of confusing money with wealth…Real wealth, of course, consists in what is produced and consumed: the food we eat, the closes we wear, the houses we live in…Inflation throws a veil of illusion over every economic process.

For the country as a whole cannot get something without paying for it. Inflation itself is a form of taxation. It is perhaps the worst possible form, which usually bears hardest on those least able to pay…Inflation "discourages all prudence and thrift. It encourages squandering, gambling, reckless waste of all kinds…It tears apart the whole

---

[36] GDP = the gross domestic product, the total market value of all final goods produced in a country. GDP is commonly used to gauge the health of a country's economy.

fabric of stable economic relationships.

Hyperinflation

In our country we are not yet experiencing hyperinflation, but it has become a problem in some countries, when inflation has gotten out of control. With hyperinflation prices go up at alarming rates. Hungary holds the current record for hyperinflation – in 1946 their prices were doubling in less than sixteen hours – and the daily inflation rate hit 195%.

The most recent example of runaway inflation was Zimbabwe in 2007-2008. Their hyperinflation hit a 98% daily rate, and prices were doubling every twenty-five hours.

Needless to say a society cannot maintain those rates for very long without all sorts of negative repercussions. In these scenarios people are incentivized to change their shopping behavior drastically – often desiring to be paid as often as once or twice a day, so that they can shop often – before the prices have a chance to increase again. (Imagine if the price of your milk increased so much that you needed to buy it twice a day!)

All of this should help us understand how much our standard of living is tied to how many hours we must work to provide for our needs and wants, not strictly how much money we possess.

The Great Depression

It seems like the Great Depression comes up whenever talk turns to recessions and depressions. Keynesians see the Great Depression as an example of the free market failing, claiming that it was caused by an overall drop in demand. Supposedly that drop required government intervention in the form of spending through massive deficits to correct. Austrians saw the Great Depression as a result of government intervention, not the free market. They believe that what President Roosevelt did prolonged the depression that the monetary policies of the Federal Reserve had been causing.

The brief timeline in **Appendix #8** should make the government intervention before and during the Great Depression clearer. Watch for the meddling with trade, taxes, supply and demand, and more.[37]

---

[37] There is a wonderful booklet on the Great Depression available on www.Fee.org, Great Myths of the Great Depression.

Lesson Thirty-Six – Too Big To Fail?

Contrary to what we so often see today, our government does not, and should not, exist to pick winners and losers. But that's what happens when "bailouts" and "stimulus plans" enter the government's budget. (And even the subsidies we were discussing earlier.)

Corollary: "No one is too big to fail." When the government bails out a company, for instance the recent auto industry bailouts, the company can continue to make the same fiscally irresponsible decisions that got it in trouble in the first place.

I like what Albert Einstein once said in regards to that: *"Those who manage their way into a crisis are not necessarily the right people to manage their way out of a crisis."*

Albert Einstein

Hazlitt explained government bailouts this way: *"The lobbies of Congress are crowded with representatives of the X industry. The X industry is sick. The X industry is dying. It must be saved. It can be saved only by a tariff, by higher prices, or by a subsidy. If it is allowed to die, workers will be thrown into the street..."*

Over the years Congress has done exactly this at different times for the coal industry, the auto industry, and the airline industry. But it must be remembered that if the "X industry" is actually vital to society, it will survive without the help of Congress.

One argument made by supporters of a failing "X Industry" is that Congress should restrict competition - limiting others coming into this field – but if the field is already crowded, capital and labor will not flow that direction any way.

Another bailout method is subsidies, but if Congress gives the "X Industry" a subsidy, they are benefitting one portion of society at the expense of the rest of society.

As Hazlitt showed, *"The taxpayers would lose precisely as much as the people in the X industry gained."*

Additionally other industries suffer since as Hazlitt explained, *"the capital and labor are driven out of industries in which they are more efficiently employed to be diverted to an industry in which they are less efficiently employed. Less wealth is created. The average standard of living is lowered compared to what it would have been."*

Hazlitt continued with words that some would consider too harsh: *"If X Industry is shrinking or dying, why should it be kept alive by artificial respiration...It is just as necessary to the health of a dynamic economy that dying industries be allowed to die as that growing industries be allowed to grow."*

An alternative to the government choosing winners and losers is to let failing companies declare bankruptcy. There are actually two different types of bankruptcy: Chapter 7 Bankruptcy is the most common in the United States.

Under Chapter 7, the business ceases operations. Chapter 11 Bankruptcy allows a failing company to reorganize, so that it may continue to function. The creditors must approve of the reorganization, and generally allow it in hopes of recouping a larger portion of their money.

Conclusion

We have covered much ground in the last thirty-six lessons. Hopefully you now have a better understanding of the importance of price, supply and demand, as well as the law of unintended consequences and incentives, to name a few.

And hopefully you can now see the value of the free market and individual responsibility. Prime Minister Margaret Thatcher put it well when she said, *"There are individual men and women, and there are families. And no government can do anything except through people, and people must look to themselves first. It's our duty to look after ourselves and then to look after our neighbor."*

It should be clear by now that increased productivity is the secret to increasing standard of livings – and that the best way to increase productivity is through the free market.

You have seen how Keynesian economists tend to want to see more government intervention and Austrian economists want to see less, since they believe that consumers are the key to the market – not the government. (In future political discussions, remember to "follow the money.")

Hopefully your eyes won't gloss over the next time someone mentions elasticity of demand, division of labor, or central planning – since you should now have some basic understanding of those.

There are many economic topics we have not covered in this introductory level book that you may run across in the future – including business cycles and marginal utility. But when you encounter these and other topics, you should have a good foundation upon which to build.

If you haven't already read them, please take a look at the various appendices at the back of the book. There is some great information there.

Review Questions

Lesson One Review

(Includes the Introduction)

1. What does Economics deal with?
2. What is Microeconomics?
3. What is Macroeconomics?
4. What causes Scarcity?
5. What causes Shortages?
6. What are Unintended Consequences?
7. Which is often more important, what is seen or what is not seen?
8. Which economist lived in the nineteenth century: Sowell, Hazlitt, or Bastiat?

Lesson Two Review

1. What are the components of our first important triad?
2. What component of the first triad is key?
3. And the components of the second triad?

Lesson Three Review

1. What do incentives do?
2. What about disincentives?

Lesson Four Review

1. Is supply generally fixed?
2. Is demand generally fixed?
3. Does demand usually go up or down when the price goes up?
4. What do we call the demand if it doesn't change with price changes?
5. Which of the following items would be fairly elastic and which would be more inelastic and why? A Ford automobile, coffee, gas, matches, pizza, salt, soda, and toothpicks.

Lesson Five Review

1. Give two examples of entrepreneurs.
2. Do entrepreneurs generally take more or less risk than other members of society?
3. What does opportunity cost refer to?

Lesson Six Review

1. What does the Preamble to the Constitution say about economics?
2. Where in the Constitution is the first reference to taxes?
3. Which chamber (the House or the Senate) is supposed to originate bills for raising revenue?

4. Who is authorized to coin money?
5. Who may not coin money?
6. Which amendment authorized income taxes?
7. Which amendment does the concept of eminent domain come from?

Lesson Seven Review

1. What was the dominant economic philosophy in the early colonial days?
2. Who came up with the concept of the "invisible hand"?
3. What does laissez faire mean?
4. In which country did the physiocrats start the idea of a country's wealth being determined by land rather than gold and silver?
5. Who wrote *The Wealth of Nations*?
6. What did Alexander Hamilton believe about tariffs?
7. What did Karl Marx think of class struggles?
8. What did Keynes think the government needed to do during the Depression?
9. Name two Austrian economists.

Lesson Eight Review

1. How were transactions accomplished before the medium of money was developed?
2. ~~What~~ Who are the two parts to every transaction?
3. Name several things that have served as money.
4. Do banks have to keep all the money in their vaults that their customers deposit? ~~Why or why not?~~
5. Is the United States currently on a gold standard? ~~When did that change?~~
6. Do we currently have a Central Bank in the U.S.?

Lesson Nine Review
(Includes Appendix #7)

1. What did Fred Schnaubelt say was responsible for raising standards of living?
2. What did Mises say was necessary for raising standards of living?
3. Which figure typically works better to see how a country is doing from year to year and why?
4. Which figure shows in a general way how citizens in one country are doing compared to citizens in another? Why?

5. Where do North Korea and South Korea both appear on the chart? (i.e. what was the GDP per capita at the time these figures were compiled?)
6. How do Haiti and the Dominican Republic compare?

Lesson Ten Review

1. Is greed a bad thing? Why or why not?
2. Whose interest do the baker and butcher have in mind, according to Smith? Is that a good thing or a bad thing?
3. What happens when a government outlaws profits?
4. What do profits (or lack of) tell the market?

Lesson Eleven Review

1. What is meant by division of labor?
2. What has to happen without division of labor?
3. Will a society improve dramatically without division of labor? Why or why not?

Lesson Twelve Review

1. Did machinery hurt or aid the textile workers in England?
2. Did Mrs. Roosevelt think machines were the friends of workers? Why or why not?

3. Why do manufacturers spend money on machines (i.e., what are they hoping to accomplish)?
4. Do machines generally aid producers, or consumers, or both?

Lesson Thirteen Review

1. What are goods?
2. What are services?
3. What are markets?
4. What are the steps goods must follow on the way to market?
5. What are capital goods?

Lesson Fourteen Review

1. What types of capital did Smith distinguish between?
2. What were some examples Bastiat gave of types of capital?
3. Why does Hazlitt say producers invest in capital goods?
4. What did Mises see as the primary difference between advanced countries and developing countries?

Lesson Fifteen Review

1. How did Bastiat list the options for what could happen to the goods a laborer has created?
2. Who does Mises say are sovereign in a capitalist system?

Lesson Sixteen Review

1. What economic system did the Pilgrims initially practice?
2. Did Governor Bradford think it was a success or a failure?
3. Who coined the term capitalism?
4. Is freedom more prevalent in capitalist societies or socialized ones?

Lesson Seventeen Review

1. Who does the planning in a socialized economy?
2. What are some of the downfalls to central planning?
3. In a capitalist economy how are decisions made?
4. Which country was socialist, West or East Germany?
5. Which of the two Germanys prospered after World War II?

Lesson Eighteen Review

1. Which step in the market process do middlemen assist with?
2. What are the alternatives to middlemen?

Lesson Nineteen Review

1. What two areas are speculators prevalent in?
2. Do speculators assist farmers or harm them?
3. What do speculators do to supply and demand?

Lesson Twenty Review

1. How did Bastiat describe interest?
2. How did Bastiat say interest rates should be regulated?
3. Are high interest rates a bad thing? Why or why not?
4. What happens when interest rates are kept artificially low?
5. Does saving cause depressions?

Lesson Twenty-One Review
(Includes Appendix #4)

1. According to Bastiat, which came first, property or laws? Why is that distinction important?
2. What did Marx believe about property rights?
3. What happens (or fails to happen) when property rights are not protected?
4. How did the Pilgrims resolve "the tragedy of the commons"?
5. What did Bastiat see as the way many people would avoid the trouble of work if given the opportunity?
6. What did Bastiat see as the role of the law?
7. Who wrote, "Government is the great fiction, through which everybody endeavors to live at the expense of everybody else."?

Lesson Twenty-Two Review

1. Does it matter if laws came before liberty and property, or if liberty and property came first? Why or why not?
2. What danger does Bastiat see when laws are not respected?
3. What problems did Bastiat believe the U.S. had in the early 19th century?

Lesson Twenty-Three Review

1. What did Friedman credit with improving standards of living?
2. Does Friedman argue that people should start at the same place or finish the same? What is the important difference?
3. What did Presidents Kennedy and Coolidge have to say about high tax rates?

Lesson Twenty-Four Review

1. What is the result of "public service"?
2. Does arguing against something being done by the government equate to arguing against it being done at all?
3. Where does the money for public projects come from?

Lesson Twenty-Five Review

1. Did Franklin want to see the government providing for all the needs of the poor?
2. What does the Declaration of Independence promise us about happiness?
3. What did Jefferson think most bad governments looked like?
4. Did Bastiat believe the government could be a universal physician or provide an unlimited treasure?

Lesson Twenty-Six Review
(Includes Appendix #6)

1. Looking at the chart, determine in what year average revenues last surpassed average outlays.
2. When did we see the largest gap between outlays and revenues?
3. Do you think Jefferson would have approved of the increasing federal debt? Why or why not?
4. How many cabinet members did President Washington have? Did President Lincoln have?
5. Which department was added most recently and why?
6. After the Defense Department, which department has the largest budget?
7. Which department has the smallest budget?

8. If you were in charge of the national budget, which department would you want to see cut the most and why?

Lesson Twenty-Seven Review

1. Are risks evil? Why or why not?
2. What happens when the government risks taxpayer money instead of private citizens taking the risks?
3. Did President Reagan think the government should protect us from ourselves?

Lesson Twenty-Eight Review

1. What is competition?
2. Why is competition a good thing?
3. When do we usually hear cries of price gouging?
4. What do monopolies do to competition and what is the result?
5. Are anti-trust laws a good thing or a bad thing? Why?

Lesson Twenty-Nine Review

1. What do price floors do to supply?
2. What is an example of price floors?
3. What do price ceilings do to demand?
4. What is an example of price ceilings?

Lesson Thirty Review

1. Are minimum wages an example of price floors or price ceilings?
2. What happens when minimum wages are set too high?
3. Do most minimum wage earners "get stuck" earning minimum wages forever?

Lesson Thirty-One Review

1. What are people describing when they speak of price gouging?
2. Are high prices after a crisis the same thing as price gouging?
3. If prices are limited (by the government) after a crisis, what are the predictable results?
4. How do higher prices reduce the problem of shortages?
5. Who did Davy Crockett come to realize should help out after a crises, the government or other individuals?

Lesson Thirty-Two Review

1. What causes the perceived need for rationing?
2. Is rationing the only option at these times?
3. What encourages black markets?
4. What are the alternatives to black markets?

Lesson Thirty-Three Review

1. What were some of the early accomplishments of unions?

2. What do unions tend to cause now?

3. What types of things do Unions tend to oppose?

Lesson Thirty-Four Review

1. What are imports?

2. What are exports?

3. Are imports bad and exports good? Why or why not?

4. Is a "balance of trade" between countries important? Why or why not?

5. What are tariffs and why do they hurt both countries involved?

6. What is outsourcing? Is it good or bad for a country?

Lesson Thirty-Five Review
(Includes Appendix #8)

1. What is GDP?

2. What often causes drops in standards of living?

3. What do some people think happens when the government prints more money?

4. Does having money equate to wealth? Why or why not?

5. What happens when hyperinflation occurs?

6. Who was president when the Great Depression began? Did he believe in laissez faire government?
7. Who initially took the United States off the gold standard?
8. When did the first minimum wage become law? What did the Supreme Court initially rule on it?
9. What does the top income tax rate top out at during the Great Depression?

Lesson Thirty-Six Review

1. What happens when the government decides that a business is "too big to fail"?
2. What happens when the government interferes to protect an "X industry" from bankruptcy or competition?
3. Who actually pays for it when a company is bailed out by the government?
4. Does bankruptcy automatically mean that a business closes its doors? Why or why not?

Economics Mid-Term

1. What is the difference between Microeconomics and Macroeconomics?

2. What causes Shortages?

3. What are Unintended Consequences?

4. What are the components of our first important triad, supply, demand and what?

5. What is the difference between incentives and disincentives?

6. Is the supply of a particular consumer good generally fixed? Why or why not?

7. Does the demand for a good generally go up or down when the price goes up?

8. What do we call demand if it doesn't change with price changes?

9. Which chamber (the House or the Senate) is constitutionally charged with originating bills for raising revenue?

10. Who does the Constitution say is authorized to coin money and who may not coin money?

11. What does laissez faire refer to?

12. How were transactions accomplished before the medium of money was developed?

13. Name several things that have served as money in the past.

14. Do banks have to keep all the money in their vaults that their customers deposit? Why or why not?

15. Who started the departure from the gold standard for the United States?

16. What is the current Central Bank in the U.S. called?

17. Does having money equate to wealth? Why or why not?

18. What happens when hyperinflation occurs?

19. Whose interest do the baker and butcher have in mind, according to Adam Smith? Is that a good thing or a bad thing?

20. What happens when a government outlaws profits?

21. What do profits (or lack of) tell the market?

22. Will a society improve dramatically without division of labor? Why or why not?

23. Did machinery hurt or aid the textile workers in England?

24. Do machines generally aid producers, or consumers, or both?

25. What economic system did the Pilgrims initially practice? Did Governor Bradford think it was a success or a failure?

26. Who coined the term capitalism? Was it a positive or a negative term?

27. Is freedom more prevalent in capitalist societies or socialized ones?

28. Who does the planning in a socialized economy? What are some of the downfalls to central planning?

29. In a capitalist economy how are decisions made?

30. Which country was socialist, West or East Germany? Which of the two Germanys prospered after World War II?

Economics Final Exam

1. What two areas are speculators prevalent in?

2. How did Frederick Bastiat describe interest and how did he say interest rates should be regulated?

3. Are high interest rates a bad thing? Why or why not?

4. According to Bastiat, which came first, property or laws? Why is that distinction important?

5. How did the Pilgrims resolve "the tragedy of the commons"?

6. Does Friedman argue that people should start at the same place or finish the same? What is the important difference?

7. What did President Kennedy have to say about high tax rates?

8. Does arguing against something being done by the government equate to arguing against it being done at all?

9. Where does the money for public projects come from?

10. What does the Declaration of Independence promise us about happiness?

11. Did Bastiat believe the government could be a universal physician?

12. Which department was added to the federal government most recently and why?

13. What happens when the government risks taxpayer money instead of private citizens taking the risks?

14. Did President Reagan think the government should protect us from ourselves?

15. Why is competition a good thing?

16. When do we usually hear cries of price gouging?

17. Are high prices after a crisis the same thing as price gouging?

18. What do price floors do to supplies?

19. What do price ceilings do to demand?

20. What is an example of price ceilings?

21. Are minimum wages an example of price floors or price ceilings?

22. Are minimum wages a good thing? Why or why not?

23. Who did Davy Crockett come to believe should help out after a crises, the government or individual?

24. Is rationing the only solution to shortages?

25. What were some of the early accomplishments of unions?

26. What are imports? What are exports?

27. What is meant when people refer to a "balance of trade"?

28. What are tariffs and how do they hurt both countries involved?

29. What is outsourcing? Is it good or bad for a country?

30. Who actually pays for it when a company is bailed out by the government?

Appendix #1 Wealth of Nations: Division of Labor

Adam Smith wrote this important chapter in 1776, and the truths are as valid today as they were then.

The greatest improvements in the productive powers of labour, and the greater part of the skill, dexterity, and judgment, with which it is anywhere directed, or applied, seem to have been the effects of the division of labour....The division of labour, however, so far as it can be introduced, occasions, in every art, a proportionable increase of the productive powers of labour.

The separation of different trades and employments from one another, seems to have taken place in consequence of this advantage. This separation, too, is generally carried furthest in those countries which enjoy the highest degree of industry and improvement; what is the work of one man, in a rude state of society, being generally that of several in an improved one.

In every improved society, the farmer is generally nothing but a farmer; the manufacturer, nothing but a manufacturer. The labour, too, which is necessary to produce any one complete manufacture, is almost always divided among a great number of hands. How many different trades are employed in each branch of the linen and woolen manufactures, from the growers of the flax and the wool, to the bleachers and smoothers of the linen, or to the dyers and dressers of the cloth!

...It is the great multiplication of the productions of all the different arts, in consequence of the division of labour, which occasions, in a well-governed society, that universal opulence which extends itself to the lowest ranks of the people. Every workman has a great quantity of his own work to dispose of beyond what he himself has occasion for; and every other workman being exactly in the same situation, he is enabled to exchange a great quantity of his own goods for a great quantity or, what comes to the same thing, for the price of a great quantity of theirs. He supplies them abundantly with what they have occasion for, and they accommodate him as amply with what he has occasion for, and a general plenty diffuses itself through all the different ranks of the society.

Observe the accommodation of the most common artificer or daylabourer in a civilized and thriving country, and you will perceive that the number of people, of whose industry a part, though but a small part, has been employed in procuring him this accommodation, exceeds all computation.

The woollen coat, for example, which covers the day-labourer, as coarse and rough as it may appear, is the produce of the joint labour of a great multitude of workmen. The shepherd, the sorter of the wool, the wool-comber or carder, the dyer, the scribbler, the spinner, the weaver, the fuller, the dresser, with many others, must all join their different arts in order to complete even this homely production.

How many merchants and carriers, besides, must have been employed in transporting the materials from some of those workmen to others who often live in a very distant part of the country? How much commerce and navigation in particular, how many ship-builders, sailors, sail-makers, rope-makers, must have been employed in order to bring together the different drugs made use of by the dyer, which often come from the remotest corners of the world?

What a variety of labour, too, is necessary in order to produce the tools of the meanest of those workmen! To say nothing of such complicated machines as the ship of the sailor, the mill of the fuller, or even the loom of the weaver, let us consider only what a variety of labour is requisite in order to form that very simple machine, the shears with which the shepherd clips the wool.

The miner, the builder of the furnace for smelting the ore, the feller of the timber, the burner of the charcoal to be made use of in the smelting-house, the brickmaker, the bricklayer, the workmen who attend the furnace, the millwright, the forger, the

smith, must all of them join their different arts in order to produce them.

Were we to examine, in the same manner, all the different parts of his dress and household furniture, the coarse linen shirt which he wears next his skin, the shoes which cover his feet, the bed which he lies on, and all the different parts which compose it, the kitchen-grate at which he prepares his victuals, the coals which he makes use of for that purpose, dug from the bowels of the earth, and brought to him, perhaps, by a long sea and a long land-carriage, all the other utensils of his kitchen, all the furniture of his table, the knives and forks, the earthen or pewter plates upon which he serves up and divides his victuals, the different hands employed in preparing his bread and his beer, the glass window which lets in the heat and the light, and keeps out the wind and the rain,

with all the knowledge and art requisite for preparing that beautiful and happy invention, without which these northern parts of the world could scarce have afforded a very comfortable habitation, together with the tools of all the different workmen employed in producing those different conveniencies;

if we examine, I say, all these things, and consider what a variety of labour is employed about each of them, we shall be sensible that, without the assistance and co-operation of many thousands, the very meanest person in a civilized country could not be provided, even according to, what we very falsely imagine, the easy and simple manner in which he is commonly accommodated." [38]

---

[38] See *I, Pencil*, available on www.fee.org for a modern tale of division of labor.

Appendix #2 The Pilgrims Try Communism

Governor Bradford wrote of their experience in his book, *Of Plymouth Plantation*:

So they began to think how they might raise as much corn as they could, and obtain a better crop then they had done, that they might not still thus languish in misery. At length, after much debate of things, the Governor (with the advice of the chiefest amongst them) gave way that they should set corn every man for his own particular, and in that regard trust to themselves; in all other things to go on in the general way as before.

"And so assigned to every family a parcel of land, according to the proportion of their number for that end, only for present use...for it made all hands very industrious, so as much more corn was planted then other ways would have been by any means the Governor or any other could use, and saved him a great deal of trouble, and gave far better content...

The experience that was had in this common course and condition...was found to breed much confusion & discontent, and retard much employment that would have been to their benefit and comfort. For the young men that were most able and fit for labour and service did repine that they should spend their time & strength to work for other men's wives and children, without any recompense. The strong, or man of parts, had no more in division of victuals & clothes, then he that was weak and not able to do a quarter the other could; this was thought injustice.

The aged and graver men to be ranked and equalized in labors, and victuals, clothes, etc., with the meaner and younger sort, thought it some indignity & disrespect unto them. And for men's wives to be commanded to do service for other men, as dressing their meat, washing their clothes, etc., they deemed it a kind of slavery... And would have been worse if they had been men of another condition. Let none object this is men's corruption, and nothing to the course itself. I answer, seeing all men have this corruption in them, God in his wisdom saw another course fitter for them.

Appendix #3 Bastiat Asks Are Politicians Greater Than Us?

"This tendency of the human race, it must be admitted, is greatly thwarted, particularly in our country, by the fatal disposition, resulting from classical teaching, and common to all politicians, of placing themselves beyond mankind, to arrange, organize, and regulate it, according to their fancy."

"…In general, however, these gentlemen, the reformers, legislators, and politicians, do not desire to exercise an immediate despotism over mankind. No, they are too moderate and too philanthropic for that. They only contend for the despotism, the absolutism, the omnipotence of the law. They aspire only to make the law." And through the law, as Bastiat demonstrates, they work to accomplish their will, not necessarily the will of those they were elected to represent.

"…One of the strangest phenomena of our time, and one which will probably be a matter of astonishment to our descendants, is the doctrine which is founded upon this triple hypothesis: the radical passiveness of mankind, --the omnipotence of the law, -- the infallibility of the legislator: this is the sacred symbol of the party which proclaims itself exclusively democratic. It is true that it professes also to be social. So far as it is democratic, it has an unlimited faith in mankind. So far as it is social, it places it beneath the mud." And here we are many generations later, seeing much of the same thing!

"…But when once the legislator is duly elected, then indeed the style of his speech alters. The nation is sent back into passiveness, inertness, nothingness, and the legislator takes possession of omnipotence. It is for him to invent, for him to direct, for him to impel, for him to organize. Mankind has nothing to do but to submit; the hour of despotism has struck.

"And we must observe that this is decisive; for the people, just before so enlightened, so moral, so perfect, have no inclinations at all, or, if they have any, they all lead them downwards towards degradation." Isn't this what we see in the United States now?

"And yet they ought to have a little liberty!" claim the politicians. But when we push for our liberty and ask *"What sort of liberty should be allowed to men?"* we are treated to their concerns: *Liberty of conscience? But we should see them all profiting by the permission to become atheists.*

"Liberty of education? But parents would be paying professors to teach their sons immorality and error; besides, if we are to believe M. Thiers, education, if left to the national liberty, would cease to be national, and we should be educating our children in

the ideas of the Turks or Hindus, instead of which, thanks to the legal despotism of the universities, they have the good fortune to be educated in the noble ideas of the Romans.

"Liberty of labour? But this is only competition, whose effect is to leave all productions unconsumed, to exterminate the people, and to ruin the tradesmen.

"The liberty of exchange? But it is well known that the protectionists have shown, over and over again, that a man must be ruined when he exchanges freely, and that to become rich it is necessary to exchange without liberty.

"Liberty of association? But, according to the socialist doctrine, liberty and association exclude each other, for the liberty of men is attacked just to force them to associate. You must see, then, that the socialist democrats cannot in conscience allow men any liberty, because, by their own nature, they tend in every instance to all kinds of degradation and demoralization." And what a price we pay for giving up our liberties!

Bastiat goes on to ask the question we should ask of our legislators: *"...The pretensions of organizers suggest another question, which I have often asked them, and to which I am not aware that I ever received an answer: Since the natural tendencies of mankind are so bad that it is not safe to allow them liberty, how comes it to pass that the tendencies of organizers are always good?*

"Do not the legislators and their agents form a part of the human race? Do they consider that they are composed of different materials from the rest of mankind? They say that society, when left to itself, rushes to inevitable destruction, because its instincts are perverse. They pretend, to stop it in its downward course, and to give it a better direction. They have, therefore, received from heaven, intelligence and virtues which place them beyond and above mankind: let them show their title to this superiority. They would be our shepherds, and we are to be their flock. This arrangement presupposes in them a natural superiority, the right to which we are fully justified in calling upon them to prove." Have they proved their natural superiority to you? They have not proven it to me.

"You must observe that I am not contending against their right to invent social combinations, to propagate them, to recommend them, and to try them upon themselves, at their own expense and risk; but I do dispute their right to impose them upon us through the medium of the law, that is, by force and by public taxes....To presume to have recourse to power and taxation, besides being oppressive and unjust, implies further, the injurious supposition that the organizer is infallible, and mankind incompetent."

Appendix #4 Bastiat Speaks of Legalized Plunder

"…Government is the great fiction, through which everybody endeavors to live at the expense of everybody else…Government is not slow to perceive the advantages it may derive from the part which is entrusted to it by the public. It is glad to be the judge and the master of the destinies of all; it will take much, for then a large share will remain for itself; it will multiply the number of its agents; it will enlarge the circle of its privileges; it will end by appropriating a ruinous proportion.

"But the most remarkable part of it is the astonishing blindness of the public through it all. When successful soldiers used to reduce the vanquished to slavery, they were barbarous, but they were not absurd. Their object, like ours, was to live at other people's expense, and they did not fail to do so. What are we to think of a people who never seem to suspect that…plunder…is no less criminal because it is executed legally and with order; that it adds nothing to the public good; that it diminishes it, just in proportion to the cost of the expensive medium which we call the Government?

"…It is radically impossible for it to confer a particular benefit upon any one of the individualities which constitute the community, without inflicting a greater injury upon the community as a whole….

"Thus, the public has two hopes, and Government makes two promises--many benefits and no taxes. Hopes and promises, which, being contradictory, can never be realized….

"These two promises are forever clashing with each other; it cannot be otherwise. To live upon credit, which is the same as exhausting the future, is certainly a present means of reconciling them: an attempt is made to do a little good now, at the expense of a great deal of harm in future. But such proceedings call forth the specter of bankruptcy, which puts an end to credit.

"What is to be done then? Why, then, the new Government takes a bold step; it unites all its forces in order to maintain itself; it smothers opinion, has recourse to arbitrary measures, ridicules its former maxims, declares that it is impossible to conduct the administration except at the risk of being unpopular; in short, it proclaims itself governmental." How prophetic were Bastiat's words…. Is this not exactly what we see today?

Appendix #5 Government: Universal Physician? Unlimited Treasure?

As we said previously, Bastiat pulled no punches when he described government and what it can and cannot accomplish: *"I should be glad enough, you may be sure, if you had really discovered a beneficent and inexhaustible being, calling itself the Government, which has bread for all mouths, work for all hands, capital for all enterprises, credit for all projects, oil for all wounds, balm for all sufferings, advice for all perplexities, solutions for all doubts, truths for all intellects, diversions for all who want them, milk for infancy, and wine for old age—*

"which can provide for all our wants, satisfy all our curiosity, correct all our errors, repair all our faults, and exempt us henceforth from the necessity for foresight, prudence, judgment, sagacity, experience, order, economy, temperance and activity…

"…Indeed, the more I reflect upon it, the more do I see that nothing could be more convenient than that we should all of us have within our reach an inexhaustible source of wealth and enlightenment--a universal physician, an unlimited treasure, and an infallible counselor, such as you describe Government to be…

"…For no one would think of asserting that this precious discovery has yet been made, since up to this time everything presenting itself under the name of the Government is immediately over-turned by the people, precisely because it does not fulfill the rather contradictory conditions of the program." Can it be better put than the way Bastiat put it? And 160 years later Government is no more successful than it was then!

He continued, *"…But let us go to the root of the matter. We are deceived by money. To demand the co-operation of all the citizens in a common work, in the form of money, is in reality to demand a concurrence in kind; for every one procures, by his own labour, the sum to which he is taxed.*

"Now, if all the citizens were to be called together, and made to execute, in conjunction, a work useful to all, this would be easily understood, their reward would be found in the result of the work itself.

"But, after having called them together, if you force them to make roads which no one will pass through, palaces which no one will inhabit, and this under the prefect of finding them work, it would be absurd, and they would have a right to argue, 'with this labour we have nothing to do; we prefer working on our own account.'"

Appendix #6 Money, Power, and Control

Most families operate under some sort of a budget, even if it's as simple as "the spending stops when the checking account is empty." Or possibly one with numerous categories where we have figured out our needs and priorities and allocated our funds accordingly.

A nation's budget is like the latter, though the upper limits work even less as a limiting factor than in a family situation. Most of us have a good idea what the categories in a family's budget look like: Housing, Food, Transportation, Medical, and Entertainment might come quickly to mind. But what are the primary categories in our country's budget?

I found that list quickly enough. It included some similar looking titles, like Housing and Urban Development, Agriculture, and Transportation. But when I did a short lesson on the federal budget recently with my high schoolers I ran into difficulty trying to determine what those categories encompassed. What exactly does the Department of Interior do? Or the State Department? How much money does each of these departments spend and how much do they need? As we looked at the departments we also arrived at a larger question – where did all these departments come from and what was their Constitutional basis? A search through Article 1, Section 8 brought us backing for some, but not all, of the departments.

Before continuing, I will admit to a bit of ignorance on my part – I knew of these executive departments and I knew of Presidential Cabinets – but I had never connected the two. I know, I know. How did I miss that little fact? I'm sure I knew it at one point – but it was only while preparing this lesson for my students that it all came together.

President Washington

So on the off chance that any of you share my ignorance let me give a little background: From George Washington's day forward Cabinets have consisted first of the men (and then the men and women) who head these various executive departments.

George Washington's Cabinet consisted of four cabinet members, Abraham Lincoln's had seven in 1862, and 150 years later, in 2012, Barrack Obama's had more than twenty. It's probably safe to say that the size of the federal government has grown along with the Presidents' Cabinets!

President Lincoln and His Cabinet July 1862

President Obama and His Cabinet July 2012

Back to the departments themselves: Our first department, the Department of Foreign Affairs, went back to the days of the Articles of Confederation. (It was renamed the Department of State in 1789.) The most recent department we've added was the Department of Homeland Security, added after the 9/11 attacks.

Surprisingly, or maybe not so surprisingly, the actual budget figures are difficult to find, even with the power of the internet at our fingertips. For those who might be interested in what I dug up, I'm including each department in descending order of one of their last budget amounts (based on the 2012 figures I found). I've also included a brief summary of their self-claimed mission statements. I hope you find those as interesting as I did. Again, as you read over them, you may want to ponder which ones actually sound Constitutional to you!

Recent Budget
The Defense Department, $530.5 billion, *"Coordinate and supervise all agencies and functions of the government concerned directly with national security and the United States Armed Forces."*

Department of Health and Human Services, $78.3 billion, *"In charge of agencies constituting the Public Health Service and Family Support Administration."*

Education Department, $67.4 billion, *"Establish policy for, administer and coordinate most federal assistance to education, collect data on U.S. schools, and* *enforce federal educational laws regarding privacy and civil rights."*

Veterans Affairs, $58.5 billion, *"Provide services and benefits for veterans."*

Department of State, $43.8 billion, *"Advance freedom for the benefit of American people and international community by helping build and sustain a more democratic, secure, and prosperous world composed of well-governed states that respond to the needs of their people, reduce widespread poverty, and act responsibly within the international system."*

Homeland Security, $39.7 billion, *"Prepare for, prevent, and respond to emergencies, particularly terrorism."*

Housing and Urban Development, $38.2 billion, *"Create strong, sustainable, inclusive communities and quality affordable homes for all."*

Justice, $27.2 billion, *"Enforce the law and defend the interests of the U.S. according to the law; ensure public safety against threats foreign and domestic; provide federal leadership in preventing and controlling crime; seek just punishment for those guilty of unlawful behavior; and ensure fair and impartial administration of justice for all Americans."*

Energy, $26.3 billion, *"Ensure America's security and prosperity by addressing its energy, environmental and nuclear challenges through transformative science and technology solutions."*

Agriculture, $22 billion, *"Provide leadership on food, agriculture, natural resources, rural development, nutrition, and related issues based on sound public policy, the best available science, and efficient management."*

Transportation, $13.7 billion, *"Serve the United States by ensuring a fast, safe, efficient, accessible, and convenient transportation system that meets our vital national interests and enhances the quality of life of the American people, today and into the future."*

Treasury, $13.2 billion, *"Maintain a strong economy and create economic and job opportunities by promoting the conditions that enable economic growth and stability at home and abroad, strengthen national security by combating threats and protecting the integrity of the financial system, and manage the U.S. Government's finances and resources effectively."*

Labor, $13.2 billion, *"Foster, promote, and develop welfare of wage earners, job* seekers, and retirees of the U.S.; improve working conditions; advance opportunities for profitable employment; and assure work-related benefits and rights."

Interior, $11.3 billion, *"Protect America's natural resources and heritage, honor our cultures and tribal communities, and supply the energy to power our future."*

Commerce, $7.7 billion, *"Promote job creation and improved living standards for all Americans by creating an infrastructure that promotes economic growth, technological competitiveness, and sustainable development."*

Brief Timeline of Cabinets/Departments

1781
The Department of Foreign Affairs is created under the Articles of Confederation.

1789
The U.S. Constitution is ratified by eleven states, establishing the Executive Branch, which includes the President of the United States and his officers/cabinet.

George Washington is sworn in as the first President of the United States. His cabinet will include four members, including the Attorney General.

The Department of War is established. (Exists until 1949 – see Department of Defense.)

The Department of Foreign Affairs is renamed the Department of State.

The Department of Treasury is established.

1798
The Department of the Navy is established. (Exists until 1949 – see Department of Defense.)

1829
The Post Office Department is established.

1862
The Department of Agriculture is established.

1870
The Department of Justice is established.

1903
The Department of Commerce and Labor is established.

1913
The Department of Labor is established as a separate department from the Department of Commerce.

1930
The Department of Veterans Affairs is established.

1947
The Department of the Air Force is established. (Exists until 1949 – see Department of Defense.)

1949
The Department of Interior is established.
The Department of Defense is established (combining Departments of War, Navy, Air Force).

1953
The Department of Health, Education and Welfare is established.

1965
The Department of Housing and Urban Development is established.

1967
The Department of Transportation is established.

1971
The Post Office Department is reorganized as an independent executive agency.

1977
The Department of Energy is established.

1979
The Department of Education is established as a separate department and the other is renamed the Department of Health and Human Services.

2002
The Department of Homeland Security is established.

Appendix #7 – GDP per Capita Activity
Instructions for Parent/Teacher

*Remember: These instructions are mere suggestions!
You may change as you see fit.*

1. The first times I introduced GDP to my students were after the earthquakes in Haiti and after the 2010 Winter Olympics.
2. For this lesson you can start by introducing the concept of GDP and GDP per capita. (GDP = Gross Domestic Product – i.e. the wealth of a country as a whole. But GDP per capita looks at the GDP average per person in a country.) Are students familiar with the terms and what they represent? Why would we want to use one or the other for comparing the economies of different countries? (Using GDP per capita makes it easier to compare the relative wealth of the "average" person in each country.)
3. Have students brainstorm what countries might have the highest GDP per capita and which might have the lowest. (We wrote their answers on the white board as they came up with them.) Where do they think their own country will fall in a list of over 200 countries in the world? (Answers will vary on these, of course. They will be able to see the answers when they receive their charts.)
4. Now pass out the "GDP per capita Charts." For this part of the activity, we used the chart that lists countries in numerical order. Have students look at them and find their own country. Do any of the highest or lowest countries surprise them?
5. For the next part of the activity students may need access to a world map, globe, or the internet: Find five countries on the list that are located in the Caribbean and highlight (or color) them with one color. (The coloring needs to be done in such a manner that the names and numbers can still be seen. As they do each color have them mark it on their key on the last page of the chart.) Then choose a second color to highlight five countries in North America (including Central America, but not including the Caribbean). Continue on to South America, Europe, Africa, Asia, and Oceania. (You may of course, do the

continents/regions in any order you want, and you may want to specify they include their own country when they get to that part of the world.)

6. Once they have highlighted countries from each region, see if they notice any trends within certain areas.
7. Next we tackled the "GDP per capita Comparison Charts." The first time we used those I let the students choose any ten of the countries they had previously highlighted. They were instructed to place one country and its GDP on each of the ten lines in the lower portion of the chart. Then they were to mark the column above each country's name to the proper height for its GDP. (You may want to show them the sample chart at this point.)
8. As part of future lessons we focused on different regions for each chart. For these lessons the students can continue to use the numerical order charts (it just requires them to search harder for some of the countries) or you may choose to give them the alphabetical list at this point. Do trends start to show up as they focus on different regions?
9. You may find other ways to use one or both of these charts. Even if you don't I'm confident that you will find your students with more understanding of GDP (and a better understanding of relative wealth) as a result!

carrabean - c

GDP Per Capita
(Based primarily on figures from the CIA World Factbook)

RANK	COUNTRY	GDP PER CAPITA
1	QATAR	102,000
2	LIECHTENSTEIN	89,000
3	MACAU	89,000
4	BERMUDA	86,000
5	MONACO	86,000
6	LUXEMBOURG	78,000
7	SINGAPORE	62,000
8	JERSEY	57,000
9	NORWAY	55,000
10	FALKLAND ISLANDS	55,000
11	SWITZERLAND	55,000
12	BRUNEI	55,000
13	ISLE OF MAN	54,000
14	UNITED STATES	53,000
15	HONG KONG	53,000
16	GUERNSEY	45,000
17	CAYMAN ISLANDS	44,000
18	NETHERLANDS	43,000
19	CANADA	43,000
20	GIBRALTAR	43,000
21	AUSTRALIA	43,000
22	AUSTRIA	43,000
23	BRITISH VIRGIN ISLANDS	42,000
24	KUWAIT	42,000
25	IRELAND	41,000
26	SWEDEN	41,000
27	ICELAND	41,000
28	TAIWAN	40,000
29	GERMANY	40,000
30	GREENLAND	39,000
31	BELGIUM	38,000

32	DENMARK	38,000
33	NEW CALEDONIA	38,000
34	UNITED KINGDOM	37,000
35	ANDORRA	37,000
36	JAPAN	37,000
37	ISRAEL	36,000
38	FINLAND	36,000
39	FRANCE	36,000
40	SAINT PIERRE AND MIQUELON	35,000
41	EUROPEAN UNION	35,000
42	SOUTH KOREA	33,000
43	THE BAHAMAS	32,000
44	SAUDI ARABIA	31,000
45	FAROE ISLANDS	31,000
46	NEW ZEALAND	30,000
47	SPAIN	30,000
48	UNITED ARAB EMIRATES	30,000
49	BAHRAIN	30,000
50	OMAN	30,000
51	ITALY	30,000
52	MALTA	29,000
53	TURKS AND CAICOS ISLANDS	29,000
54	GUAM	29,000
55	SLOVENIA	27,000
56	CZECH REPULIC	26,000
57	SEYCHELLES	26,000
58	EQUATORIAL GUINEA	26,000
59	ARUBA	25,000
60	BARBADOS	25,000
61	SLOVAKIA	25,000
62	CYPRUS	25,000
63	GREECE	24,000
64	PORTUGAL	23,000
65	LITHUANIA	23,000
66	ESTONIA	22,000
67	FRENCH POLYNESIA	22,000
68	TIMOR-LESTE	21,000

69	POLAND	21,000
70	TRINIDAD AND TOBAGO	20,000
71	HUNGARY	20,000
72	GABON	19,000
73	CHILE	19,000
74	LATVIA	19,000
75	ARGENTINA	19,000
76	ANTIQUA AND BARBUDA	18,000
77	RUSSIA	18,000
78	CROATIA	18,000
79	MALAYSIA	18,000
80	URUGUAY	17,000
81	PANAMA	17,000
82	BOTSWANA	16,000
83	SAINT KITTS AND NEVIS	16,000
84	PUERTO RICO	16,000
85	BELARUS	16,000
86	MAURITIUS	16,000
87	LEBANON	16,000
88	MEXICO	16,000
89	SINT MAARTEN	15,000
90	TURKEY	15,000
91	CURACAO	15,000
92	VIRGIN ISLAND	15,000
93	BULGARIA	14,000
94	ROMANIA	14,000
95	DOMINICA	14,000
96	KAZAKHSTAN	14,000
97	GRENADA	14,000
98	NORTHERN MARIANA ISLANDS	14,000
99	VENEZUELA	14,000
100	SAINT LUCIA	13,000
101	SURINAME	13,000
102	COSTA RICA	13,000
103	IRAN	13,000
104	ANQUILLA	12,000
105	BRAZIL	12,000

106	SAINT VINCENT AND THE GRENADINES	12,000
107	MONTENEGRO	12,000
108	SOUTH AFRICA	12,000
109	LIBYA	11,000
110	COLUMBIA	11,000
111	SERVIA	11,000
112	PERU	11,000
113	MACEDONIA	11,000
114	AZERBAIJAN	11,000
115	ALBANIA	11,000
116	ECUADOR	11,000
117	PALAU	11,000
118	CUBA	10,000
119	TUNISIA	10,000
120	THAILAND	10,000
121	CHINA	10,000
122	TURKMENISTAN	10,000
123	DOMINICAN REPUBLIC	10,000
124	COOK ISLANDS	9,000
125	MALDIVES	9,000
126	JAMAICA	9,000
127	BELIZE	9,000
128	MARSHALL ISLANDS	9,000
129	GUYANA	9,000
130	MONTSERRAT	9,000
131	BOSNIA AND HERZEGOVINA	8,000
132	NAMIBIA	8,000
133	TONGA	8,000
134	AMERICAN SAMOA	8,000
135	SAINT HELENA, ASCENSION, AND TRISTAN DA CUNHA	8,000
136	KOSOVO	8,000
137	EL SALVADOR	8,000
138	ALGERIA	8,000
139	UKRAINE	7,000

140	FEDERATED STATES OF MICRONESIA	7,000
141	IRAQ	7,000
142	BHUTAN	7,000
143	PARAGUAY	7,000
144	EGYPT	7,000
145	SRI LANKA	7,000
146	KIRIBATI	6,000
147	ANGOLA	6,000
148	ARMENIA	6,000
149	SAMOA	6,000
150	GEORGIA	6,000
151	JORDAN	6,000
152	MONGOLIA	6,000
153	NIUE	6,000
154	SWAZILAND	6,000
155	BOLIVIA	6,000
156	MOROCCO	6,000
157	GUATEMALA	5,000
158	INDONESIA	5,000
159	SYRIA	5,000
160	NAURU	5,000
161	FIJI	5,000
162	VANUATU	5,000
163	REPUBLIC OF THE CONGO	5,000
164	HONDURAS	5,000
165	PHILIPPINES	5,000
166	NICARAGUA	5,000
167	CABO VERDE	4,000
168	VIETNAM	4,000
169	INDIA	4,000
170	WALLIS AND FUTUNA	4,000
171	UZBEKISTAN	4,000
172	MOLDOVA	4,000
173	GHANA	4,000
174	TUVALU	4,000
175	SOLOMON ISLANDS	3,000

176	LAOS	3,000
177	PAKISTAN	3,000
178	WEST BANK	3,000
179	PAPUA NEW GUINEA	3,000
180	NIGERIA	3,000
181	DJIBOUTI	3,000
182	SUDAN	3,000
183	CAMBODIA	3,000
184	WESTERN SAHARA	2,500
185	KYRGYSTAN	2,500
186	CHAD	2,500
187	YEMEN	2,500
188	CAMEROON	2,500
189	TAJIKISTAN	2,500
190	MAURITANIA	2,000
191	SAO TOME AND PRINCIPE	2,000
192	LESOTHO	2,000
193	SENEGAL	2,000
194	BANGLADESH	2,000
195	THE GAMBIA	2,000
196	ZAMBIA	2,000
197	KENYA	2,000
198	NORTH KOREA	2,000
199	COTE D'IVOIRE	2,000
200	TANZANIA	1,500
201	BURMA	1,500
202	BENIN	1,500
203	BURKINA FASO	1,500
204	UGANDA	1,500
205	NEPAL	1,500
206	RWANDA	1,500
207	SOUTH SUDAN	1,500
208	SIERRA LEONE	1,400
209	HAITI	1,300
210	COMOROS	1,300
211	ETHIOPIA	1,300
212	ERITREA	1,200

213	MOZAMBIQUE	1,200
214	GUINEA-BISSAU	1,200
215	AFGHANISTAN	1,100
216	MALI	1,100
217	TOGO	1,100
218	GUINEA	1,100
219	TOKELAU	1,000
220	MADAGASCAR	1,000
221	MALAWI	900
222	NIGER	800
223	LIBERIA	700
224	CENTRAL AFRICAN REPUBLIC	700
225	BURUNDI	600
226	SOMALIA	600
227	ZIMBABWE	600
228	DEMOCRATIC REPUBLIC OF THE CONGO	400

GDP per capita Comparison Chart

GDP per capita:

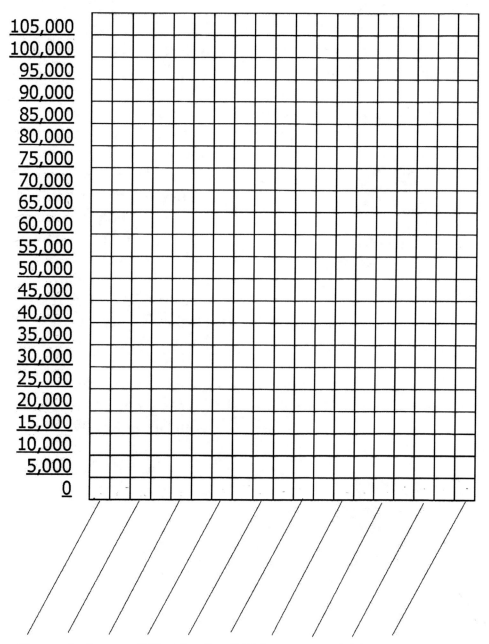

Countries with their GDP per capita

Appendix #8 Brief Timeline of the Great Depression

1923

President Warren Harding dies and Vice President Calvin Coolidge becomes President. Coolidge believes in *laissez-faire* government and announces, *"The business of America is business...Don't expect to build up the weak by pulling down the strong."*

President Coolidge

1925

Under Coolidge's administration the top tax rate is lowered to 25%.

1929

Herbert Hoover becomes President; he is not committed to *laissez-faire* government.

President Herbert Hoover

Almost half of bank loans are being used for stock market investments. In the first half of the year over 300 banks close; an "Ordinary Recession" begins in August.

There are murmurs of problems in the Stock Market on Thursday, October 24. As the market starts a downward spiral, powerful New York City bankers invest their own money heavily to help stabilize the Market. There is a slight rally on Friday, October 25, but with back-to-back drops of 12.8% and 11.7% on "Black Monday" and "Black Tuesday", the stock market officially crashes.[39] The Great Depression has begun.[40]

1930

Fifty-six percent (56%) of the U.S. population now live in urban areas.

By February the Fed has cut the prime interest rate from 6% to 4%.

Another 1,000 banks close. There is no deposit insurance at this time, so depositors lose all their money when their banks close.

---

[39] A Crash is typically defined as a loss of 20% or more in one day, or in a few consecutive days.

[40] The Great Depression will continue through April of 1942, plagued by severe price deflation and high unemployment.

Huey Long, Louisiana Governor and U.S. Senator, calls for the redistribution of the wealth from the nation's wealthiest to the poorest – he calls it "Share Our Wealth." Long's slogan is "Every Man A King." Within five years, more than seven million have joined "Share Our Wealth Clubs" across the country.

Huey Long

Over the protests of 1,028 national economists, President Herbert Hoover signs into law the Smoot-Hawley Tariff Act. The law raises tariffs (taxes) on 20,000 imported goods.

1931

In an attempt to help the financial situation of the country, the Federal Reserve raises interest rates. (Probably not a wise move at the time!)

President Hoover is blamed for the rising unemployment across the country. Shantytowns, often referred to as "Hoovervilles," spread across the country – hundreds of thousands of homeless men occupy them.

One of the many "Hoovervilles"

As the Great Depression gains speed, Great Britain becomes the first major power to go completely off of the gold standard.

Davis-Bacon is signed into law by President Herbert Hoover; the purpose is intended to prevent local firms from underbidding large national firms. (It is still on the books, and today benefits big unions more than anyone else.)

1932

Less than three years into the Great Depression, the Stock Market has fallen 91%, to 41 points. Industrial production has fallen 52% in the same period, and corporate profits have fallen 49%.

Under President Hoover, Congress creates the RFC (Reconstruction Finance Corporation), an independent government agency. Its role is to provide capital to banks, insurance companies, mortgage companies, and building and loan associations, in the form of loans from the Federal Government. (In the next twenty-five years it will buy stakes in more than 6,000 financial institutions, at a cost of more than $50 billion of taxpayer money – money that is no longer available for private uses.)

Franklin Roosevelt accepts the Democratic Party nomination at the Convention in Chicago. He ends his acceptance speech with his first reference to the New Deal that he will then work to implement:

"I pledge you, I pledge myself, to a new deal for the American people. Let us all here assembled constitute ourselves prophets of a new order of competence and of courage. This is more than a political campaign; it is a call to arms. Give me your help, not to win votes alone, but to win in this crusade to restore America to its own people."

Herbert Hoover signs into law the largest peacetime tax increase in our country's history, raising the top tax rate from 25% to 63%.

Franklin D Roosevelt handily beats Herbert Hoover in the fall presidential election, receiving 472 electoral votes to Hoover's 59.

1933

On March 4th, in his first inaugural address, President Franklin Roosevelt (FDR) tells the American people with respect to the struggling economy, *"The only thing we have to fear is fear itself."* The next day Roosevelt declares a Four-Day Bank Holiday to begin on March 6th. FDR then signs the Emergency Banking Relief Act of 1933 – prohibiting people from hoarding gold. The following week Roosevelt introduces his radio "fireside chats" to reassure the American people about the economy.

The Civilian Conservation Corps (the CCC) is created to help provide jobs for many of the country's 25% who are unemployed.

CCC workers constructing a road.

In April, Roosevelt follows Great Britain's lead and takes the American Dollar off the gold standard, making it easier for the Federal Government to inflate money. The state of New

York becomes the first of twenty-six to pass minimum price laws.

In May President Roosevelt signs the Tennessee Valley Authority Act (TVA). FDR wants TVA to be *"a cooperation clothed with the power of government but possessed of the flexibility an initiative of a private enterprise."*

Congress creates the Agricultural Adjustment Administration (AAA), the Farm Credit Administration, the Federal Emergency Relief Administration, the National Recovery Administration, and the Public Works Administration.

Congress passes the Emergency Banking Bill, the Farm Credit Act, and the National Industrial Recovery Act.

In June the Glass-Steagall Act is passed. It establishes a "wall" between investment banks and commercial banks and establishes the Federal Deposit Insurance Corporation (FDIC).

A minimum wage is enacted ($0.25 per hour) as part of the National Recovery Act. (In 1935 the Supreme Court declares the National Recovery Act unconstitutional, and the minimum wage is abolished.)

Upton Sinclair, author and socialist, writes up a 12-point plan: EPIC – "End Poverty in California."

Upton Sinclair

By the end of the year an additional 4,000 banks have failed and almost 44% of mortgages are in default. FDR signs the Home Owners Loan Act, creating the Home Owners Loan Corporation.

With its creation, Roosevelt declares, *"I feel we have taken another important step toward the end of deflation which was rapidly depriving many millions of farm and home owners from the title and equity to their property."* With a significant investment of capital from the Treasury, the agency helps over one million homeowners (20%) refinance their mortgages in the next three years, though many will eventually default on their loans anyway.

Sixty-six year old Dr. Townsend comes up with a plan, the "Townsend Old Age Revolving Pension Plan", or simply, the Townsend Plan, to have the government take care of elderly with a pension plan. Within two years, there are more than two million members in Townsend Clubs across the country trying to get the Townsend Plan passed.

In December, the 21st Amendment is ratified, ending Prohibition.

The farm bill is passed, to help starving farmers who make up 25 percent of the country at the time.[41]

1934

In a close three-way race, Upton Sinclair loses his bid for California Governor.

The Federal Reserve ("the Fed") is reorganized so it will have more financial clout, and the Federal Housing Administration (FHA) is created. The FHA insures mortgages so that more lower-income families can afford mortgages.

The SEC (U.S. Securities and Exchange Commission) is established as an independent agency responsible for enforcing federal securities laws.

President Roosevelt announces that he intends to provide a program for "Social Security."

1935

Following an idea already popularized in numerous European countries, the Social Security Act is signed into law by President Franklin D. Roosevelt. The new law creates a social insurance program to provide retired workers, 65 and older, a continuing income.

The Wagner Act passes – giving Union officials exclusive bargaining power in unionized workplaces.

The Supreme Court declares the portions of the National Recovery Act which empowered the President to regulate employment hours, wages, and minimum ages, to be unconstitutional.

Congress creates the Works Progress Administration, the National Labor Relations Board and the Rural Electrification Administration.

Congress passes the Banking Act of 1935, the Emergency Relief Appropriation Act, the National Labor Relations Act, and the Social Security Act.

The Revenue Act of 1935 brings the top income tax rate level to 75%.

---

[41] Today only two percent of Americans live on farms, and the farm subsidies that continue to be passed by Congress are mainly helping big conglomerates.

1936

The Stock Market has increased 73% in two years – back up to 180 points.

The top tax rate is raised to 79%.

1937

When the Supreme Court threatens to deal a constitutionality blow to more of FDR's programs, he threatens to expand the number of Justices on the Supreme Court so that he can get a pro-Roosevelt majority. With "a switch in time that saves nine",[42] the Supreme Court reverses itself on the minimum wage issue, and ushers in a modern era of constitutional law that allows almost limitless amounts of government intervention in the marketplace. (We can only dream of what might have been different if the Supreme Court had had a collective backbone at the time!)

Additionally the Supreme Court upholds the constitutionality of the Wagner Act. The response in the work place is a growing amount of unemployment – back to 1931 levels.

The first lump-sum payments are made to retired workers under the new Social Security.

1938

The Federal National Mortgage Association (Fannie Mae) is created by FDR – to buy mortgages from lenders, keeping some and selling the rest on the secondary mortgage market. This makes it easier for lenders to continue to make loans during the economic turmoil of the Great Depression.

1939

The top tax rate is 91%.

Adolf Hitler invades Poland, starting World War II. The United States does not enter the war for another two years, but some believe that the war efforts are what begin to bring the United States out of the Depression.

---

[42] In 1937, as today, there are nine justices on the Supreme Court.

Bibliography/Additional Reading

Some of my favorite economics books include:

Basic Economics and *Applied Economics* by Thomas Sowell
    These are two of my favorite economics books for those who want to learn more.

Economic Policy: Thoughts for Today and Tomorrow by Ludwig Von Mises
    (From transcripts of six lectures he gave in Buenos Aires, Argentina in 1959) An excellent read – Mises spelled it out clearly for his foreign audience, but it is a good tool for Americans as well.

The Economics of Freedom: What Your Professors Won't Tell You: Selected Works of Frederic Bastiat (Another small, easy read with great information.)

Lessons for the Young Economists by Robert P. Murphy (good insight for beginners)

Economics in One Lesson by Henry Hazlitt (not a short book, despite its title, but very good).

The Concise Guide to Economics by John Cox (this book is actually short, sweet, and to the point).

Romancing the Voters by Fred Schnaubelt
    A conservative commentary on politics and economics

If you are looking for more information, several of my long-time favorite economics websites are:
    Foundation for Economic Education www.fee.org
    Foundation for Teaching Economics www.fte.org
    Izzit.org (inexpensive, educational DVDs on economics) www.Izzit.org
    Wall Street Journal www.wsj.com

Glossary

- Bailout = the government giving an ailing company (read "bankrupt" or "nearly bankrupt" company) liquid assets (money or assets that can easily be sold for cash).
- Black Market = a market where the goods that are bought and sold are either illegal, or where the goods are being sold illegally (around trade restrictions, etc.).
- Chapter 7 Bankruptcy = the most common bankruptcy in the United States. Under Chapter 7, the business ceases operations.
- Chapter 11 Bankruptcy = bankruptcy where a failing company reorganizes and continues to function.
- Capital Goods (Producer Goods) = goods used in production.
- Competition = active demand for two or more goods in short supply.
- Consumer Goods = goods which are meant to be consumed.
- Deflation = a persistent reduction in the prices of goods and services, often accompanied by increased unemployment. Temporary drops in prices are not deflation.
- Depression = a severe economic downturn.
- Embargo = the partial or complete prohibition of commerce and trade with a particular country, in order to isolate it or punish it.
- Fiat Money = money that is only "valuable" because the government has declared it so, not backed by gold, silver, or any other valuable asset.
- GDP = the gross domestic product - the total market value of all final goods produced in a country.
- Gold Standard = a monetary system that uses a fixed weight of gold as the basic exchange unit.
- Goods = a material service or thing with value to others.
- Inflation = a general upward climb of prices of goods and services, causing every dollar to be worth less, because it can buy less.
- Laissez Faire = "let it be."
- Macroeconomics = "the big picture" – how things look at the national or world-wide level.
- Market = the process of exchanging goods between buyers and sellers.

- Mercantilism = the belief that a state must accumulate as much gold and silver as possible in order to be wealthy.
- Microeconomics = the behavior of the consumer and individual businesses.
- Monopoly = a single company controlling access to a particular product or service.
- Needs = those things we must have for survival – food, shelter, clothes.
- Unintended Consequences = what happens as a result of the policy that may not have been intended.
- Outsourcing = subcontracting a service, often to another country.
- Rationing = the government artificially restricting any particular raw materials, goods, or services.
- Recession = a period of general economic decline. Even among mainstream economists there is widespread disagreement as to when one actually begins.
- Scarcity = insufficient quantity of something to supply all the wants for it.
- Specialization = concentrating one's efforts on a particular activity.
- Stagflation = inflation and economic stagnation together over a long period of time.
- Tariff = A tax imposed on one or more imported products.
- Value = what something is worth to someone; i.e. what they are willing to pay.
- Wants = a desire for certain things.

About the Author

Catherine Jaime did her undergraduate work at the Sloan School of Management at the Massachusetts Institute of Technology. She has additional economics training through the Foundation for Teaching Economics and the Foundation for Economic Education. Catherine has taught in grades K-twelve with a concentration in high school economics and government. She firmly believes in the importance of the U.S. Constitution and the free market, and it shows in her writings. She has authored a number of history books and several booklets dealing with government and/or economics, including Understanding the U.S. Constitution, Constitution Topical Study, a play and novel about the Constitutional Convention, and many more.

Her other loves include *Sharing Shakespeare* and *Leonardo the Florentine*, and she has written both non-fiction and fiction books on those topics.

In her spare time she runs a homeschool resource center, Creative Learning Connection. Her books can be found in numerous places on the internet, including Amazon, CurrClick, and her own websites: www.CatherineJaime.com and www.CreativeLearningConnection.com.

CPSIA information can be obtained at www.ICGtesting.com
Printed in the USA
LVOW09s1720130716

496180LV00006B/262/P

9 781492 272649